The
Pocket

Universal
Principles of
Branding

The
Pocket

Universal Principles of Branding

100 Key Concepts for Defining, Building, and Delivering Brands
Mark Kingsley

ROCKPORT

Quarto.com

© 2025 Quarto Publishing Group USA Inc. Text © 2025 Mark Kingsley

First published in 2025 by Rockport Publishers, an imprint of The Quarto Group,

100 Cummings Center, Suite 265-D, Beverly, MA 01915, USA.

T (978) 282-9590 F (978) 283-2742

Rockport Publishers titles are also available at discount for retail, wholesale, promotional, and bulk purchase. For details, contact the Special Sales Manager by email at specialsales@quarto.com or by mail at The Quarto Group, Attn: Special Sales Manager, 100 Cummings Center, Suite 265-D, Beverly, MA 01915, USA.

10 9 8 7 6 5 4 3 2 1

ISBN: 978-0-7603-9382-6

Digital edition published in 2025
eISBN: 978-0-7603-9383-3

Library of Congress Cataloging-in-Publication Data availalbe

Page Layout: John Hall Design Group

Printed in China

For you, my colleague.

CONTENTS / ALPHABETICAL

CONTENTS / ALPHABETICAL

CONTENTS / CATEGORICAL

CONTENTS / CATEGORICAL

CONTENTS / CATEGORICAL

INTRODUCTION

Anyone operating in today's marketplace works in branding—to some degree. And anyone living in modern society is equally affected by branding. Brands inhabit our minds, influence how we see ourselves, and filter our view of the world.

This breviary concentrates an earlier collection of principles. Both this and the previous book attempt to cover the full horizon of a brand. Each section is loosely categorized and color coded (with some overlap) in the upper left corner of each spread: magenta corresponds to Defining Brand, orange to Building a Brand, and cyan to Delivering a Brand.

Hopes for this book
It is the goal for these principles to spark dialogue, reflection, and understanding, instead of being seen as a recipe book or operations manual. See them as entry points, moments to reflect, or tools to reframe preconceptions.

Ideal outcomes could include an acceptance of the foreign, the amateur, or the unexpected as brand aspects worthy of consideration. The hope is that the cumulative effect will convey a sense of permission, and perhaps a degree of liberation for all parties involved.

One aspect of creativity is "allowing" things to come into being. So, let's simply begin by saying "yes."

1 ABSTRACTION

A defining quality of human existence is a capacity for abstract thinking. We compress complex ideas into understandable expressions. And brands allow us to do it with increasing ease and increasing levels of complexity.

- Our abstractive abilities go beyond words and language.
- Photographs and films are two-dimensional abstractions of a three-dimensional world.
- If we fully enter the multiverse, we may experience abstractions of time, gravity, and being—through bodies different than the ones we're used to.
- Brands are high-level abstractions and not just physical objects. The whole identity system—logo, color palette, patterns, typography, images—compresses complex ideas and values into a shorthand.
- Brands are more than abstractions of things or ideas. They are abstractions of ways of being that are authentic to themselves.

Kellogg's Frosted Flakes is an American brand which uses the name Frosties in the UK, European Union, and Israel.

2 ANTHROPOLOGY / ETHNOGRAPHY

To better serve their audience, brands need to understand how they fit into people's lives. Big data has transformed customer and market research, but it only measures past events. Ethnography can tap into larger trends, examine any gaps in the data, or help understand the why.

- Ethnography is the localized, hands-on examination of life as it is experienced.
- Good ethnography is contextual and detailed and describes without editorializing.
- It is slow and deliberate, which is why much ethnography in the discovery phase of branding projects lacks nuance.
- Use open-ended questions, like "how do you…?"
- Correspond with subjects instead of speaking for them.

One method of ethnography is participant observation: collected notes, photographs, objects, etc. are organized into a discovery report or forecast. The resulting social theories are known as anthropology—or, in branding, the strategic upfront.

The author's photo was taken in the Tsukiji fish market as part of an ethnographic research trip to Tokyo.

3 ASSOCIATION

If I tickle your nose with a feather, where is the tickle located?

- Stimuli enters our sensory system without any attachment or meaning.
- Everything we perceive is framed by language, even if it doesn't have a name.
- We live in a world of associations.
- Those associations reflect a particular moment in culture, our lived experience, and our personal use of language.
- Logos do not represent a company upon creation. They become associated with a company with exposure over time.
- A brand is a specific node in a network of associations.
- Brands trigger associative memory, not historical memory.
- Every other point within the associative network of a brand has the potential to either build or erode its overall perception. That brand "tickle" occurs in the audience's mind—out of our control.

The question "If I tickle your nose with a feather, where is the tickle located?" illustrates a fundamental concept of phenomenology.

19

4 AUTHENTICITY

"Damascus" describes a sword that held a very sharp edge and did not shatter in battle. Its distinctive, water-like surface pattern confirmed the weapon's quality and is an early example of a brand's authenticity confirmed by a visual identity.

- Brand authenticity does not always stem from a single product.
- If computers basically focus on files, then for Apple, their delivery and storage becomes iPads, AirPods, and the iPhone.
- Beyond hardware, a method to exchange files is needed: iCloud, Apple Music, Apple ID, and Apple Pay.
- These improvements established an authenticity—confirmed by the Apple logo, much like the Damascus pattern confirmed a blade's quality.
- Because Apple's hardware established a reputation of ease-of-use and reliability, the equally easy and reliable mobile payment service is nominated into that sphere of authenticity.

The distinctive pattern
of Damascus steel
is one of the earliest
visual brand identities.

5 BANDITS AND ROBOTS

- Recommendation algorithms on digital platforms are called multi-armed bandits after casino slot machines, or "one-armed bandits." They filter metadata through methods relevant to the brand and then deliver personalized, dynamic content to users.
- Once a user arrives within a defined audience, that definition becomes more and more constrictive. And in streamed films or music, that begins to feel like a restrictive diet.
- Although the wondrous sense of discovery occurs at the edges of form and popularity, it seems that a brand's algorithmic bandits and robots pale in comparison to any recommendation (or provocation) coming from a thoughtful and informed human being.

Similar to a game of tic-tac-toe, multi-armed bandits adjust throughout all phases of the test.

6 BEAUTY, NOT BEAUTIFICATION

Beauty is not always the main goal for a brand, but it informs development and engagement.

Beauty does not follow strategic positioning. It is in tension with how brands are developed. A board of directors cannot create beauty, but it can beautify through style.

- Beautification is superficial. When things become unfashionable or depleted, the response is beautification.
- Style can be consumed, updated, and consumed again, while beauty cannot. Style is overdescribed, overfamiliar, and overconcretized, while beauty remains outside that cycle.
- The challenge for anyone working in branding is to let beauty emerge. Even if it falls outside of existing brand guidelines, or if the audience takes things to an unexpected place.
- Beauty has greater connective potential than the transactional, insistent, and captioned world of style.

Top: Much of the beauty of architect Le Corbusier's Villa Savoye in Poissy near Paris, France, is seen in the way one moves through the building and how views are revealed.

Bottom: The banality of developments found across the United States comes from building styles that are overdescribed, overfamiliar, and overconcretized.

7 THE BIG FIVE

One way to analyze a brand's audience is with The Big Five Personality Traits, easily remembered as the acronym OCEAN: openness, conscientiousness, extraversion, agreeableness, and neuroticism.

- Openness is eagerness to try new experiences and ideas.
- Conscientiousness is associated with people who are thoughtful, plan ahead, and exercise good impulse control.
- Extraversion (the opposite of introversion) measures how comfortable one is around others.
- Agreeableness is manifested through kindness, charitable behavior, and affection.
- Neuroticism describes one's response to stress and uncertainty.

Most brand communication appeals to fight-or-flight or pleasure: fear/security, acquisition, or the attraction of sexual partners. This seems impoverished and relegated to the id.

Today's algorithmically powered environment offers potential for more nuanced, psychologically complex messages—ideal opportunities for brands to contribute to a richer social environment.

Secured by

ADT®

1.800.369.0996

Markers like this one for ADP home alarm systems, as seen in the Ditmas section of Brooklyn, are directed towards feelings of security and the fear of death.

8 BLACK BOX OR SCIENTIFIC METHOD

Branding client fees can be enhanced by maintaining a degree of mystery, or promoting a proprietary "branding process." Mystery adds intrigue and sexiness. Expertise and professionalism add comfort.

- More cynical designers see these brand processes as a way to professionalize the "black box" of design.
- Following a series of proprietary steps establishes client expectations, offers benchmarks for accountability, and tracks progress.
- A clearly defined method helps clients accept the vagueness of creativity.
- But one can go through a professional process and still come out with a bad branding system.

A professional practice is designed to create professional results. But effective results don't always come from such an environment. The challenge is to engage all possibilities, regardless of where they come from.

1 UNIFY

2 SIMPLIFY

3 AMPLIFY

Ken Carbone, Cofounder and Chief Creative Director of the Carbone Smolan Agency, follows the clearly defined method of Unify, Simplify, and Amplify.

9 BLURRING

- Today we live in the blur. "Borders" between brands and brand associations are more porous than ever.
- All of a sudden, it is not so strange for Louis Vuitton to collaborate with Supreme on co-branded luggage.
- Such collaborations are meeting points where widely divergent brands coexist equally.
- Blurring opens up territory beyond a brand's basic activity.

Categories have blurred to where a transportation company, Uber, owns no vehicles. And Airbnb, a hospitality company, owns no property.

Blurring confirms that brands are nothing more than associations. As we entertain multiple ideas simultaneously, we entertain multiple brand associations as well.

- Brands are a symbolic system that helps bind society together.
- We speak through brands.
- And brands help us speak a complex language in a complex time.

A red denim Louis Vuitton/Supreme jacket, designed by Louis Vuitton's menswear artistic director, Kim Jones, with the collaboration blurred seamlessly.

BODY AND BRAND

- A brand's visual and verbal expressions are the easiest qualities to reproduce.
- They are merely representations of the brand—not the brand.
- A brand experience happens in a body, in space, in time. This means that it occurs in a context that can be adjusted or enhanced.
- A way to approach this opportunity is to think about how things shift: moving from dark to light, deadened acoustic space into a more active environment, or from carpet onto hardwood floors.
- Vanilla-scented candles were originally used by Morgans Hotel Group. Spaces managed by anyone who worked for Morgans, or the subsequent Ian Schrager Company, have a vanilla scent.
- Techniques like these can subtly energize a space and any brand associations attributed to the experience.

A predominate vanilla scent hung in the air of the now-closed Gramercy Park Hotel's lobby.

BRAND ARCHITECTURE

Growth brings complexity. As the number of employees increases, opportunities become more varied, opinions (both internally and externally) diversify, and, with all that, the "architecture" of the brand becomes noisier.

- Even if divisions are logical offshoots, when grouping and managing them becomes difficult, reorganization is needed.
- This is known as a brand architecture project.
- Brand architecture gives structure and clarity to both internal and external audiences.
- This, in turn, can prepare a company for the current (and future) marketplace.
- Brand architecture is as much internal social engineering as organizational design.
- The new structure requires the emotional investment of all stakeholders.

FedEx's brand architecture reflects a "branded house" strategy, where each division logically links to the main company.

BRANDS ARE A TECHNOLOGY

Since Apple is regarded as an ideal brand, it's easy to think that its technological products define the brand. Actually, their brand is a technology.

- Simply put, technology is a means to an end—it is how we effect change on objects in the world.
- Therefore, technology extends our bodies. A hammer extends our arm; a telescope, our vision; and the wheel, our range.
- What technology extends our lived experience? Language.
- Language is probably humanity's greatest technology.
- Since brands use a collection of languages, both visual and verbal, then branding can be seen as a technology as well.
- The technology of branding extends more than just one individual's lived experience; it is a proposal—an extension— of a way to live.

Top: Apple store by the Chicago River in Chicago.

Bottom: Apple store in Liberty Square, Milan. Two locations separated by an ocean, but united by an aesthetic point of view.

13 BRANDED UNCONSCIOUS

Photography has altered how we understand the world, both consciously and unconsciously. We no longer need to see things in person in order to believe.

- This idea of a photographic/optical unconscious comes from the German critic Walter Benjamin.
- Building upon this, is there such a thing as a branded unconscious?
- Photographs and films allow us to experience distant events or events that happen too slowly or quickly to perceive.
- In a way, they bring us closer.
- So perhaps brands bring us nearer to an ideal.
- Brands allow us to occupy, charge, or approach varieties of feelings in a shorthanded way.
- As we speak a language without thinking, we "speak" brands in a similarly unconscious manner.

This 1878 series of images by English photographer, Eadweard Muybridge, revealed how a galloping horse's hooves did not continually touch the ground; thus expanding our perception of the world. Today brands have a similar revealing effect.

"Branding" means different things to different people and, consequently, ends in different results. Branding can be done by advertising firms, and advertising can be done by branding firms, often through campaigns.

- "Advertising" and "branding" are often used interchangeably.
- Advertising works within a shorter time frame.
- Branding works across years.
- A common metaphor is a clock face divided into three sections: 12 to 4 is prepurchase, 4 to 8 is purchase, 8 to 12 is postpurchase.
- This is often called the "customer journey." Branding covers all areas of the clock.
- Prepurchase is the domain of advertising: building awareness, differentiating, motivating action.
- Prepurchase is development and production.
- Purchase is moving from "buy me" to "take me home."
- Postpurchase is tech support, returns, or problem resolution.

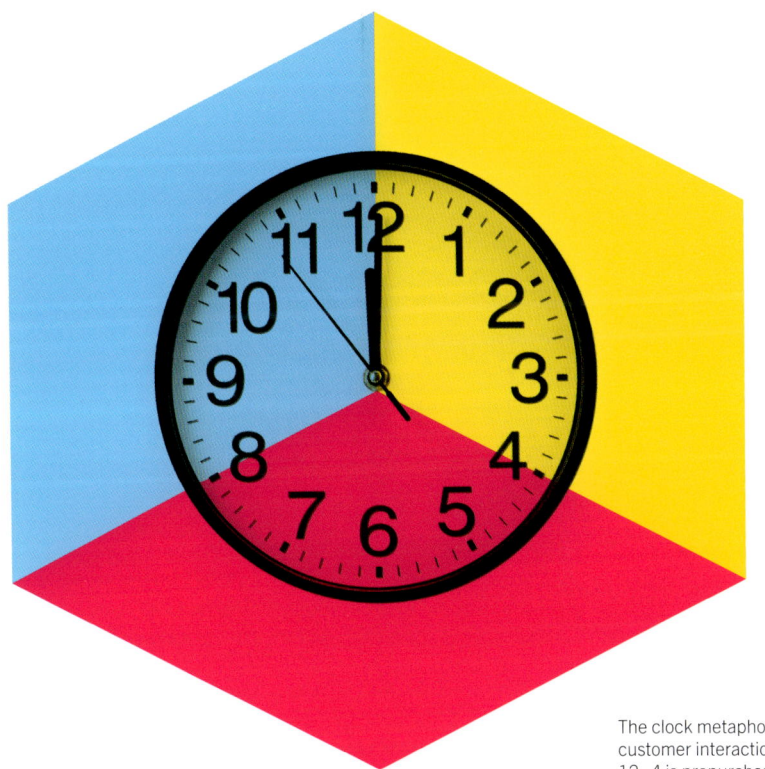

The clock metaphor of
customer interaction.
12–4 is prepurchase,
4–8 is purchase, and
8–12 is postpurchase.

CASE STUDIES

Brand professionals tend to work within the case study model, developed at the Harvard Business School in the 1920s.

- Case studies analyze crisis moments in a business history by identifying root causes, actions taken, and ensuing results.
- Studying history may seem like an appropriate approach, but there are inherent flaws.
- All history is the result of an imposed narrative.
- The presence of financial data may suggest objectivity, but in reality there is no objectivity.
- Crisis moments come from a series of influences, and require a rigorous and genealogical investigation.
- Proper analysis can draw from any field, as long as it is appropriate to the topic.
- So, why not move beyond the case study model?
- Why not open our apertures to sociological, anthropological, psychological, philosophical, or other theoretical models?
- Shouldn't brand professionals regard brands from as many angles as possible?

The Harvard Business
School. Birthplace of
the case study model.

In 1958, author Theodore Sturgeon came to a revelation: "Ninety percent of everything is crud."

- Sturgeon's Law is especially applicable when looking at advertising.
- This includes celebrity advertising: both the easiest path to client approval and the laziest form of professional practice.
- There needs to be a logical connection between celebrity and brand.
- The brand ambassador is a level where thinking of one immediately evokes the other.
- Audrey Hepburn's relationship with Givenchy is the gold standard of brand ambassadorship.
- This model has devolved into a ritual where celebrities are robotically asked who they are wearing during red carpet events.
- A curious trend is celebrity as brand creative director: Justin Timberlake at Bud Light Platinum, Alicia Keys at BlackBerry, Lady Gaga at Polaroid—unless it's rapper and cannabis expert Snoop Dogg unveiling Leafs By Snoop, relinquishing product development to a celebrity is rarely a good strategy.

Rapper and cannabis expert, Snoop Dogg, is the owner of the Leafs By Snoop line of medical and recreational marijuana-related products.

A common trope in branding is to describe the practice as "storytelling." But this thinking reduces things to a procedural level.

- In storytelling, it is better to write a plot where a character struggles or transforms.
- The more engaging a character, the more it "sticks." Many of us know a Ferris Bueller type, or have stumbled into a situation like Forrest Gump.
- Human beings are hardwired for character.
- We see faces or patterns in ambiguous fields, whether they be visual or behavioral, in a phenomena known as "pareidolia."
- Those patterns are the building blocks of character.
- Character helps navigate personal relationships.
- Perhaps it is best to think of brands as character-driven.
- Allowing a brand to develop a character allows for flexibility as markets and audiences change—while maintaining continuity. The essence and expectations of that character can remain stable as the world around it changes.

Pareidolia is the phenomenon where human beings see faces or patterns in ambiguous fields.

COMFORT AND DISRUPTION

Of all modalities of branding, much attention goes to disruption. This conforms with the idea that to be noticed, a brand needs to stand out dramatically from the competition—either by opening up new markets or exploiting profit margin differences.

- If brands are psychological connections, then they need to conform to the customer's life by making them feel comfortable.
- Comfort is the background against which innovation appears.
- Comfort is the expectation of sensory continuity, where we expect things to be generally the same as they were previously. Anything counter to expectations is disruption.
- We speak the language of others, not one of our own invention. That connection is comfortable.
- Trusted brands relieve anxiety by adopting a common language—aesthetics, usage, behavior, etc.—and fitting comfortably into the customer's life. Their introduction may have been disruptive, but their longevity derives from comfort.
- The tension between comfort and disruption is constantly changing.

Top: Door knobs were standard hardware in the United States for a century.

Bottom: After the Americans with Disabilities Act of 1990, the door lever displaced the door knob and has become the preferred choice.

19

COMMIT TO THE BIT

Besides real-life experience in building and presenting brands, one can build the skill of "selling" a brand in other venues. One effective method is improvisational acting.

- "Improv" has no pre-written script. Each agrees to accept each other's proposals, and to be in the moment.
- Everyone has to commit to the bit—this means to develop the world being created as much as possible, imagining oneself as an authentic inhabitant, and engaging without hesitation.
- Like learning the guitar and branding, the act of *doing* helps one learn improv. And one gets better by doing it often.
- The only way to prepare beforehand is to read, listen, and see as much as possible: history, economics, politics, culture, art, etc.
- Improv—and (obviously) branding—is not about one thing; it is about everything. The more references one draws from, the richer the palette, the better the outcome.

Dumb Starbucks in Los Angeles, California, was a 2014 project by comedian Nathan Fielder, which explored the fair use of copyrighted material as parody.

20

CONFLICT

Conflict seems to be the very nature of the universe, even down to the atomic level. The Latin roots of "cogitate" (to think) and "conflict" (to oppose) are similar. Cogitate from "co-" (together) and "agitare" (to shake); conflict from "co-" and "fligere" (to strike).

- The best ideas are revealed in meeting, clashing, and disagreeing.
- Such interactions do not need to be acrimonious.
- Conflict can be constructive, but only when participants are honest, receptive, and able to see criticism as a gift.
- Conflict stemming from dissatisfied customers may be the result of a faulty design or standard, and may become a stimulus for growth.
- This way, conflict—a basic human experience—becomes an important ingredient in the articulation, development, and delivery of a brand.
- Embraced as a resource, conflict leads to solutions, revealing the nature of anything from audience desire, the state of the market, the competitive set, and even the brand itself.

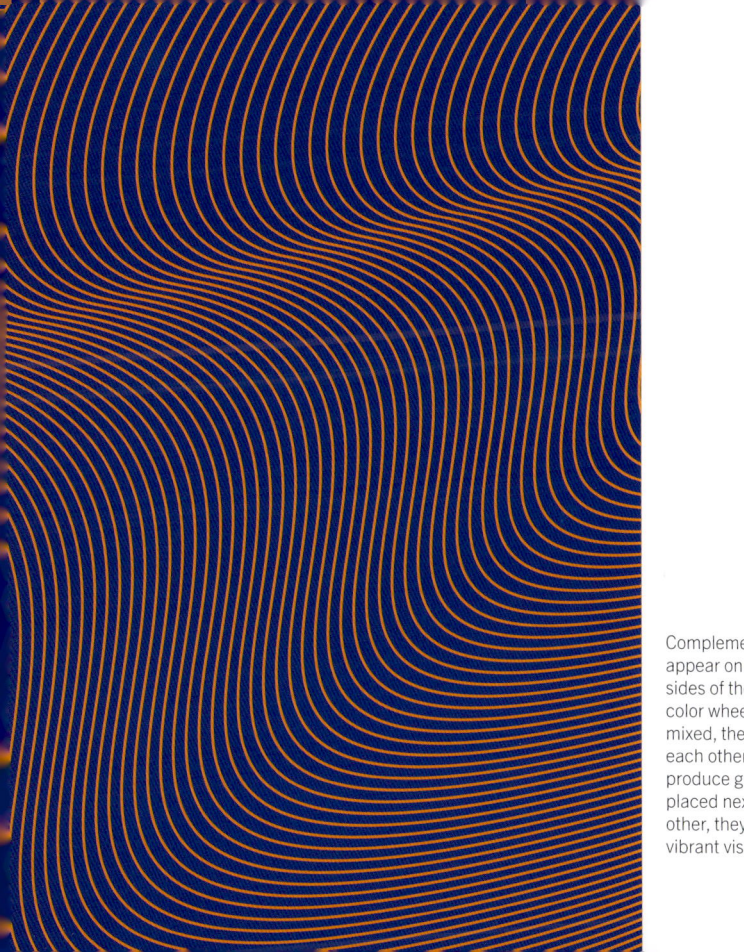

Complementary colors appear on opposite sides of the traditional color wheel. When mixed, they cancel each other out and produce gray. When placed next to each other, they can create vibrant visual effects.

Simply put: branding is a discipline where practitioners analyze existing contexts, then develop new contexts that their clients may authentically and distinctively inhabit.

- Branding is a discipline born from, and operating out of, vagueness.
- There seems to be no limits to its territory.
- All human, and at times nonhuman, behavior sits within the purview of branding.
- The general view of branding speaks about attracting and maintaining customers while maintaining a unique identity. While correct, it overly focuses on results and returns on investment.
- We are more than just shoppers.
- This is a world of branded objects. Our context is brands.
- We speak in brands, surround ourselves with brands, decide through brands, and set life goals aided by brands.
- As branding's territory expands, so does the number of contexts.
- Beyond the marketplace, there are linguistic, political, technological, sociological, and aesthetic ramifications to the presence of brands in contemporary culture.

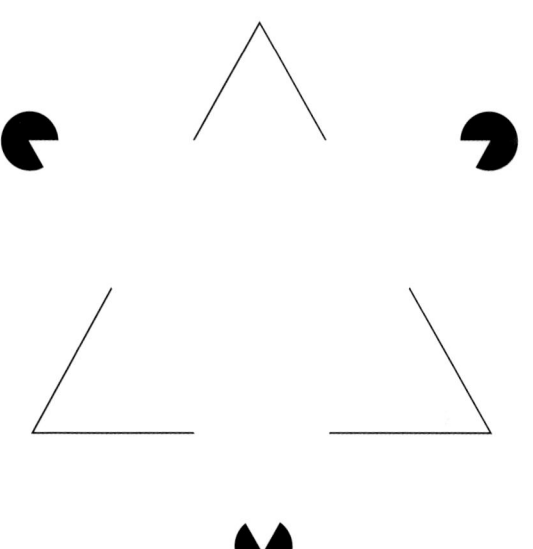

The Kanizsa triangle, named after the Italian psychologist and artist Gaetano Kanizsa, evokes a white shape in a vague context.

- If brands are the expression of interdisciplinary activity, then the people who develop, build, distribute, and maintain those brands need to be as un-siloed as possible.
- Job titles and definitions create efficiencies, but they also give people excuses to not participate in the brand's full development.
- The problem is that people are siloed according to their tasks.
- But what if we saw people by how they experience and interpret the world?
- In this case, everyone's "craft" becomes the filter through which they contemplate the larger world.
- "I do not believe that I am mastering the craft so much as I am allowing the craft to explain … the workings of the universe and the connections that make the universe flow." — Letterpress artist Amos Paul Kennedy Jr.
- This approach expands the collective team, and reminds us that the product of our work is what mediates human relationships.

Amos Paul Kennedy Jr.'s "Proceed and Be Bold!" poster; as seen in the author's collection.

57

CUSTOMER JOURNEY

One of the most fundamental tools in branding is the customer journey, which describes the transformation from potential customer to purchaser, user, and then, ideally, an advocate.

- Measuring these steps against brand offerings helps develop touchpoints that guide people through this process.
- The tool shifts focus toward customer experience and defines goals for each interaction.
- There may be variations in steps or names, but the customer journey follows a standard pattern.
  - First is awareness of the brand.
  - Then a person learns more about the brand.
  - The next step is the transaction: purchasing, signing up, or becoming a member.
  - Depending on the product or service, there may be a customer service or resolution step.
  - Ideally, the journey could then transition into advocacy.
- While a powerful framework, try not to see the customer journey as a transactional progression—it is more of a rough guide than a perfect recipe.

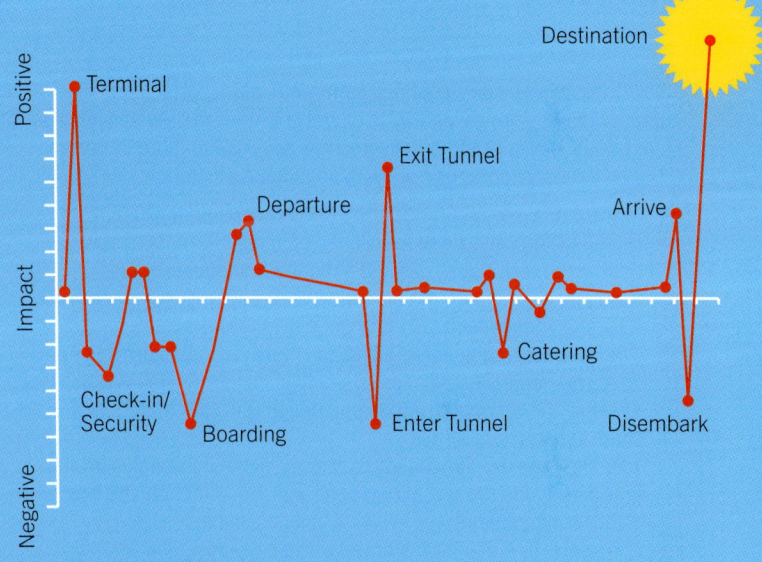

Positive

Impact

Negative

Terminal

Check-in/
Security

Boarding

Departure

Enter Tunnel

Exit Tunnel

Catering

Arrive

Disembark

Destination

A version of Oxford
Corporate Consultants'
1998 customer journey
map for Eurostar.

Physical objects that were once common—maps, video cameras, paper tickets—are giving way to digital counterparts. As this process continues, how a brand is delivered has never been more important. Digital delivery concerns itself with speed and efficiency.

- In the digital realm, brands need to consider load time.
- Digital brands also need to balance changing formats of new devices. Smartphones created a mobile-first approach to webpage design, and the next widely adapted delivery system will have the same effect.
- The death of traditional retail means more packages arriving on consumer doorsteps.
- Physical delivery can surprise and delight through materiality, shifts in texture, or smell.
- To make them less appealing to thieves, some companies print graphics inside the box. When done well, the effect can be like discovering treasure.
- The goal is to enhance the brand without seeming like a marketing exercise, like including a coupon for future purchases.

Who Gives a Crap packages their bamboo-based toilet paper in decorative wrapping and puns. The only plastic used is the tape that seals the shipping box.

25

DIFFERENCE AND DIFFÉRANCE

There is no meaning to anything other than the one we attribute.

- Strategy is often defined as deliberate differentiation.
- Gold does not mean "rich" or "luxury;" it is just gold.
- Meaning comes from our anthropomorphic projection on a chaotic universe; probably built off of binary differences like near/far, bigger/smaller, dark/light, hot/cold, etc.
- Brands mean nothing in and of themselves.
- Meaning derives from use and the associations ascribed to them.
- French philosopher Jacques Derrida used the word "différance"—a play on the similarities of the French words for "differ" and "defer." For him, deferred meaning described the ongoing play of signifieds and signifiers, an active field requiring branding practitioners to listen differently—beyond the transactional—where brands become a dialogue.
- In this model, difference becomes a handle that our consciousness can grasp. An assist rather than an insist.

The philosopher, Gilles Deleuze, offers an interesting way of thinking about brands. "Instead of something distinguished from something else, imagine something which distinguishes itself."

26

DIGITAL TO SOCIAL STRATEGIST

With the Internet age, the role of strategist split between the Harvard Business School case study model and the new, exotic digital strategist—both having responsibilities that continue to be difficult to define.

- The division between a "traditional strategist" and digital strategist is false. Both analyze situations and propose responses. It's all strategy.
- If one were to create a subspecialty, perhaps there's room for a social strategist. It wouldn't be a trend forecaster but more like tracking the reverberations of vibe shifts across society.
- The social strategist would expand their observations through psychological, philosophical, and sociological models. The people who do similar work today are known as cultural critics and public intellectuals.
- A good critic places phenomena in culture, which seems to align nicely with branding.
- Given the speed of culture today, this seems even more relevant.

A sampling of critics and intellectuals whose work traces the reverberations of society.
Top row, left to right: Malcolm Gladwell, Li Edelkoort, Walter Benjamin
Bottom row, left to right: Slavoj Žižek, Susan Sontag, Douglas Rushkoff

27

DISAGGREGATED DATA

One of the analytical tools of the COVID-19 pandemic was the generation and usage of rich data.

- Aggregated data produces an easy-to-understand number when setting public policy, but pandemics affect different subpopulations differently.
- Aggregated data doesn't always offer nuance, which could best direct a targeted, preventative response.
- That requires disaggregated data, gathered at the individual level, and filtered to accurately represent populations by neighborhood, income/education level, ethnic origin, etc.
- The largest branding and advertising holding companies engage in market research based on disaggregated data.
- Each brand insights group has its own individualized group of factors tracking shifts across ranges of populations.
- While both forms of data are essential to understanding brands within market contexts, all data needs to be interpreted with sensitivity. This is the difference between observation and insight.

Aggregated data does not fully reveal the focused details of relations or context.

28

DO NO HARM

Any tool, whether instrument or method, is inherently neutral. It has no ambition, is indifferent to its application, and maintains no ethical stand.

- In the late 1980s, the phrases "product branding" and "branding" had explosive growth in usage.
- Since then, the practice of branding has matured and become more effective.
- Branding techniques can either be used to better understand consumer needs or specifically target advertising, to promote human existence or to destroy the fabric of civil society.
- Branding can only exist if there is an audience.
- Common sense suggests that everyone in branding should direct their efforts towards the continued presence of that audience.
- A good place to start is to redefine the rationale for most brand development, which is profit.
- What if we expanded that definition beyond profit and considered how branding could address multiple flows of ecological, social, and health transactions.
- This could have a market-expanding effect.

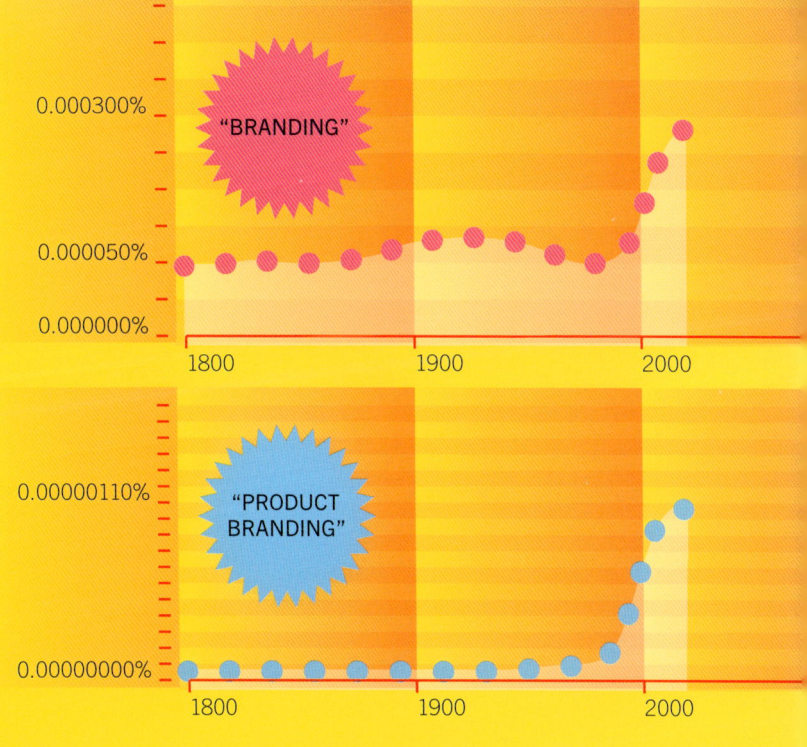

Results from Google's Ngram Viewer for the phrases "branding" (top) and "product branding" (bottom).

29

DON'T FEAR THE AUDIT

The word "audit" carries negative connotations due to its use in accounting and taxes. But an audit is a powerful tool in the development and management of a brand.

- Once a brand grows into new markets, or to a point where there are too many touchpoints for an easy evaluation, regular brand audits become a management necessity.
- Audits have to be balanced with regional specifics. For example, Japanese banks present gifts to new customers, while banks in the United States no longer do.
- Additionally, a competitive audit including other brands may identify best practices.
- Multiregional or global brand audits can be part of a company-wide unification effort.
- The ideal result of a well-executed audit is a coherent brand, appropriate for local audiences, the best example being Sesame Street. Characters are different across markets, but the basic lessons of human dignity remain the same.

Top: The characters Bert and Ernie on the original American television show *Sesame Street*.

Bottom: The character Baaji on *SimSim Humara*, the Pakistani version of *Sesame Street*.

In the mid-twentieth century, graphic design systems were the building blocks of corporate identity. One started with a logo, selected a typeface and color palette, arranged it all in a consistent manner, then applied that look and feel to stationery, the sides of trucks, signage, and so on. The design system helped identify an organization, while the organization's goods, services, and behaviors impacted how the general public felt about it.

- Information technology changed how we view design.
- Businesses saw design as a tactic within a brand system.
- Corporate identity designers then pushed beyond the creation of a perfect artifact into the creation of an ecosystem intended to "hang together" into the mental response we now call a "brand."
- Feelings, in all their ambiguity, are now as important to a brand as a good logo, if not more so.

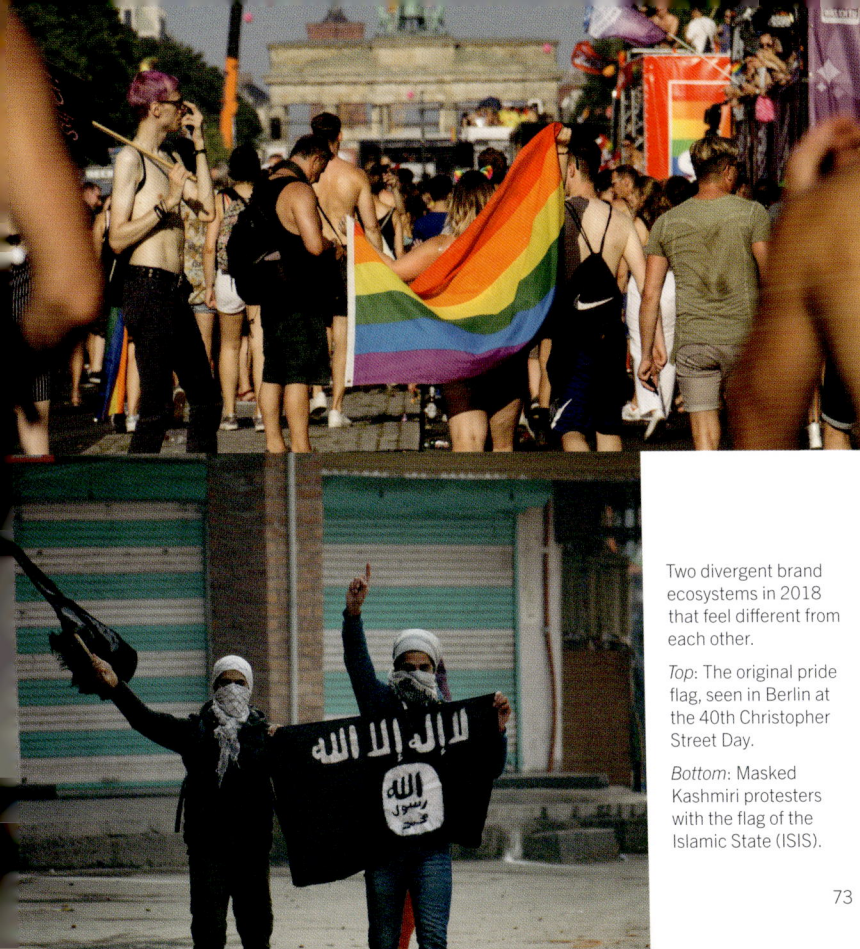

Two divergent brand ecosystems in 2018 that feel different from each other.

Top: The original pride flag, seen in Berlin at the 40th Christopher Street Day.

Bottom: Masked Kashmiri protesters with the flag of the Islamic State (ISIS).

73

31

ENGAGEMENT

While conversations about brands focus on the audience, employee engagement—aligning employees to a brand's values and personality—is a crucial factor. It ensures consistency across all customer interactions and reinforces brand associations.

- The traditional first step is to define the brand's values.
- Each decision made by, and for, the company is measured against those values.
- Sometimes brand values are distilled into a purpose statement.
- How would the purpose statement influence the packaging and delivery of products? How does it apply to the hiring process? Or when an employee leaves the company?
- Employee engagement is extremely important and worth continual reinforcement.
- Unfortunately, it is frequently streamlined into a one- or two-day "onboarding."
- The goal is to have employees "be" the brand without having to "think" the brand first.
- Then customers feel they're dealing with an attentive human being, instead of someone reading off of a script.

Actively aligning all levels of employees to a brand's values and personality ensures consistency across customer interactions, reinforces brand associations, and may help build efficiencies.

32

ENVIRONMENT / ANTI-ENVIRONMENT

Philosopher and media theorist Marshall McLuhan described the transformed reality resulting from new technologies as "environment." Our attention eventually numbs to the pervasiveness of these environments, so McLuhan described anything helping us perceive them as "anti-environment."

- McLuhan's tetrad of effects may be useful in understanding a brand's effect on culture.
- Arrange four diamonds in an X, with the object being studied in the center.
- Then, place four questions in each of the diamonds:
  - Upper left: What does it enhance?
  - Lower right: What does it obsolesce?
  - Lower left: What does it retrieve from earlier obsolescence?
  - Upper right: What does it reverse into when pushed to the limits of its potential?

The tetrad applied to any smartphone shows that it:

- Enhances Internet accessibility and aids in memory.
- Makes a number of things obsolete: older phones, maps, tickets, etc.
- Retrieves the camera and written communication (texting).
- May (ironically) reverse interpersonal communication.

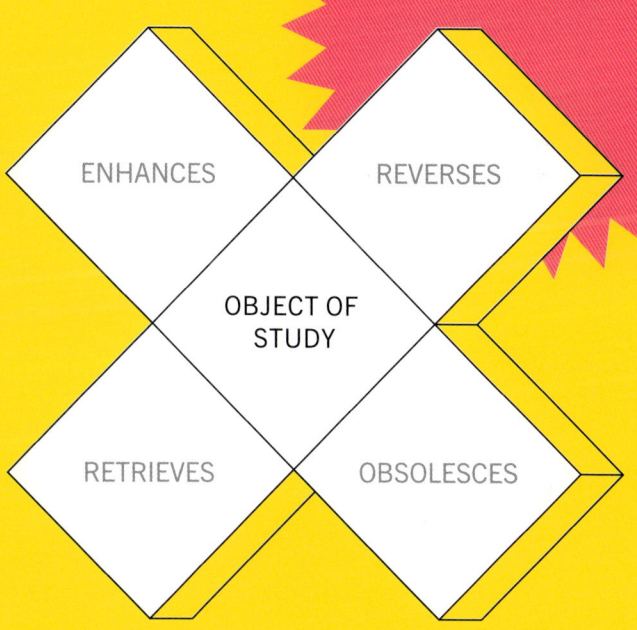

ENHANCES

REVERSES

OBJECT OF STUDY

RETRIEVES

OBSOLESCES

Marshall McLuhan's tetrad of media effects.

33

EROTICS OF BRANDS

When presenting, work agencies frequently feel compelled to explain creative work. Logic seems to be the way to make work digestible for clients—and ultimately worth paying for.

- But is the creative work allowed to exist, and connect, on a purely aesthetic, sensual level?
- "Erotics" comes from Eros, the Greek god of passion and fertility, and refers to the sexual, the creation of life.
- An example of a brand accommodating an erotics would be Restoration Hardware's Manhattan flagship.
- Anyone is welcome to use the furniture . . . hang out, have a meeting, or sit down and finish a presentation.
- Restoration Hardware created a space and then stepped back to see what happens. They made a conscious decision to observe and listen to people, whether they be customers or not.
- They allowed for unexpected creativity and life—in other words, a brand erotics.

Restoration Hardware's New York City flagship allows visitors to enter, sit on the furniture, and just be.

34

EVERYBODY LIVES IN A BODY

Much of our creative efforts are directed toward an ideal, which is then reframed as "normal." But "normal" is a statistical average applied to the largest section of the population. Normal is a convenience.

- There is always tension between the ideal and reality.
- At some point in life, our bodies no longer conform to the statistically normal.
- If not congenital or present at birth, we all eventually diminish by disease and aging.
- There is a growing conversation about accessibility for those outside the statistically normal.
- We are only beginning to fully appreciate the neurological, physical, and cognitive diversity that exists alongside the more visible ethnic and sexual diversities.
- This is another opportunity for brands to establish stronger, more empathetic connections with their audience.
- It requires brands to prioritize sustained relationships and accommodate the reality of how people truly live in their bodies, in time.

Dr. Dan Formosa evaluates kitchen devices and offers design adjustments in his online video series.

35

EVERYONE WORKS IN BRANDING

Today, it seems that "branding" is the new topic-du-jour. When Kim Kardashian repeatedly speaks about "my brand," that idea has reached full saturation in the collective consciousness.

- Tracking brand perception has never been easier, as is the ability for the public to affect brands in response.
- With social media, online reviews, and the ability for everyone to host YouTube programming, the audience has never had more power.
- So, in a sense, everyone does work in branding, whether intentionally or not.
- Brands attempt to measure this "output" through varieties of research and tracking.
- One of the foremost metrics is the Net Promoter Score (NPS).
- NPS asks two questions: "How likely are you to recommend [company]?" and "Why?"
- Given that brands are associations built over time, they should view their audience in a much more nuanced way. Because the audience is an equal partner in a brand's success.

A wax figure of American television personality, Kim Kardashian, at Madame Tussauds London.

The slang term "flexing" ("to show off") has almost doubled in usage over the past couple decades. Perhaps it's a condition of social media, the growth of communications technology, but there seems to be a collective acceptance of ostentatiousness.

- When brands flex, the outsized nature of the flex grates against associations that they have spent so much effort in building.
- Determining this is more a matter of degree.
- Spanish luxury fashion house Balenciaga's collaboration with the American footwear company Crocs is one stunt that solidifies each company's respective position on the luxury/casual spectrum.
- The list of misguided brand extensions launched an exhibition known as the Museum of Failure.
- There are many humorous examples: Harley-Davidson's perfume, wine coolers, and ties; or Colgate's Beef Lasagna.
- None of these brand extensions seemed logical, and they all reached beyond expectations, with various degrees of hubris.

Spanish fashion house Balenciaga's collaboration with the American footwear company Crocs resulted in products like this boot.

37

FRAMEWORKS

Frameworks are mental structures that expedite the analysis of markets and organizations, and offer beginning steps in defining or managing a brand.

- Useful frameworks offer comparative criteria, and lead to actionable insights.
- But these insights are never neutral. The intentions and needs of the developers are always present, ultimately coloring results.
- Frameworks are often expressed as a diagram or verbal phrase.
- Once the framework has been agreed upon, it is used in day-to-day operations, employee evaluations, and future decisions.
- In all cases, brand frameworks manifest utopian thinking.
- And because these frameworks are the products of biased decisions, there will always be a divisive element present.
- Now that brands are being increasingly drawn into larger cultural dialogues—and using that dialogue to virtue-signal their position—the tried-and-true frameworks that built the profession are due for serious reevaluation.

One well-known expression of utopian thinking from the 1960s, adapted to a typical pyramid framework.

38

FRAMING

Brands contribute to how we construct meaning, often by defining what are known as semantic domains.

- A semantic domain is a specific shared set of meanings within a given context but with differences in particular details.
- Examples include the familial (father, mother, child), body-oriented (head, shoulders, waist, feet), or social (CEO, vice president, director, assistant). Each word within a domain is learned in relation to each other.
- Semantic domains may build connections between brands and consumers. For example, when describing different shapes of wine bottles, we can point to the bottle's neck, shoulder, and foot.
- Brands can also frame a fuzzier, more poetic function.
- For example, a shopping cart full of produce and unprocessed food can now be called a TikTok shopping cart because of all the TikTok content on healthy eating.

The semantic domain of Starbucks eschews small, medium, and large for tall, grande, and venti.

39

GATHERING (AND DIVIDING)

The general conversation about brands speaks about how they gather the like-minded together. While lofty, it doesn't fully consider how brands can also divide people.

- Trucks, biscuits, and blue jeans are all brands.
- So are religions, political parties, and social movements.
- Even the Islamic State (ISIS) is a brand.
- As brands now feel pressured to take stands on cultural or political topics, the difficulty in avoiding a misstep increases.
- The widespread adoption of Toyota trucks by extremist groups like ISIS or the Taliban forced Toyota in 2022 to include a clause in sales contracts that any new Land Cruiser could not be resold within a year. This was done to prevent any potential violations of foreign exchange laws—and to keep their products out of any propaganda videos.
- This all reveals that brands are not, and cannot, be neutral.

A Toyota vehicle with Palestinian fighters on their way to military exercises in the southern Gaza Strip, December 2021.

40

GENEROSITY (AND HUMILITY)

A brand requires more than one person to exist. It is, in effect, a social dialogue.

- If one works in branding, it may be beneficial to see users "and, audiences" as an artistic medium, like canvas, rather than as a resource to be exploited.
- This is not an argument for total altruism, but at least a plea to begin with a degree of generosity.
- Designers can practice generosity by thinking of their work as a gift to someone they have not yet met. It could be usability, affordability, accessibility, humor, or even plain beauty.
- The gift then becomes a means of connection.
- In order for a brand to establish some rapport, there has to be humility, beginning with listening and leading to trust.
- Brands need an audience willing to be open to the brand's proposition; and the best way to achieve that is to begin from a generous spirit.

In 1990 Smart Design partnered with OXO International to develop the influential OXO Good Grips line, which introduced the concept of Universal Design to mass retail, and created consumer demand for better-performing, easier-to-use kitchen tools.

41

GO OUTSIDE YOUR LANE

When searching for branding innovation, look to smaller, independent firms. They are less beholden to profit-and-loss lines, have more hiring flexibility, and respond to change with more agility.

Independent firms have more latitude in defining their process, allowing employees to "swim outside their lane." Borders are opened out of necessity rather than prescription.

- One common overlap is when designers work in brand strategy.
- With enough experience, and a sharp intellect, there's nothing to say that a designer can't make a valuable strategic contribution.
- But it's more problematic when a strategist or client manager makes a suggestion to the design team.
- The development of a designer inculcates them into a subculture built on taste and judgment, which can easily separate them from other disciplines.
- As an alternative to taste, why not develop an appetite? Taste is restrictive while appetite is inclusive.

Innovation comes from blurring professional
categories and developing new fields of practice.

42 HAPTICS

Interaction through touch is known as haptics. And it is an often-overlooked, or neglected, channel during the design process. This is because the visual is often more likely to be given primacy over the haptic.

- Physical stimuli continually speaks to us, both directly through our neurology and indirectly through lived experience and memory.
- The skin is the largest organ in the body, the largest sensory receptor, and the point where we begin to comprehend the world.
- Haptic information communicates mass, weight, and momentum in a way in which verbal and visual methods can only symbolize.
- Physical brands have a unique opportunity to convey "authenticity" by attending to even the smallest detail: the crispness of a corner on a folding carton, or a secure click on a garment closure.

Jean-Baptiste Carpeaux's sculpture, *Ugolino and His Sons*, depicts the effect of fingers pressing into flesh; an effect famously attributed to Michelangelo.

43

HEARING VOICES

Up until now, brands have relied on visual systems to distinguish themselves. And the introduction of digital assistants hints at a future where brands speak with their own voice and personality.

- One can imagine voice-based assistants with distinctive accents and ways of speaking.
- If brands have personalities, then this is the next step toward a more dimensional character and a specifically defined audience.
- Linguistic flourishes like Cockney rhyming slang, French verlan, or even pig latin could express a brand's spirit.
- The first hurdle to verbal interaction is the usual corporate fear of wanting to be distinctive but not too distinctive.
- The second hurdle is the gatekeepers of the device and operating system's developers.
- Any brand-specific assistant would be measured against both community and developer standards.
- These sorts of controls shouldn't be seen as a limit but rather as creative stimulus.

FAST SAUSAGE & MASH
PLEASE SELECT AMOUNT
(MAXIMUM DISPENSE £50)

LADY GODIVA
<(£5)

SPECKLED HEN
<(£10)

COMMODORE
<(£15)

HORN OF PLENTY
<(£20)

PONY
(£25)>

DIRTY
(£30)>

DOUBLE TOP
(£40)>

NIFTY
(£50)>

Certain cash points in east London allow users
to select Cockney rhyming slang as the language
of choice.

44

HETEROGENEITY

Heterogeneity across different studies is a constant presence in data. This is the inconsistency of results, not due to chance, stemming from varying approaches in the study's design; or there may be statistical differences between studies.

- Data does not exist on its own. We make it. And truth does not emanate from data objectively.
- Combining studies, known as a meta-analysis, improves overall precision by increasing the generalizability of individual study results, answering questions not posed in the individual studies, settling differences between studies, or generating new hypotheses.
- Results from a meta-analysis seem to be better because the process outweighs individual studies, but these results aren't necessarily more reliable. The results capture what happened, not necessarily what is happening.
- If there is excessive heterogeneity, the validity of the meta-analysis is in question.

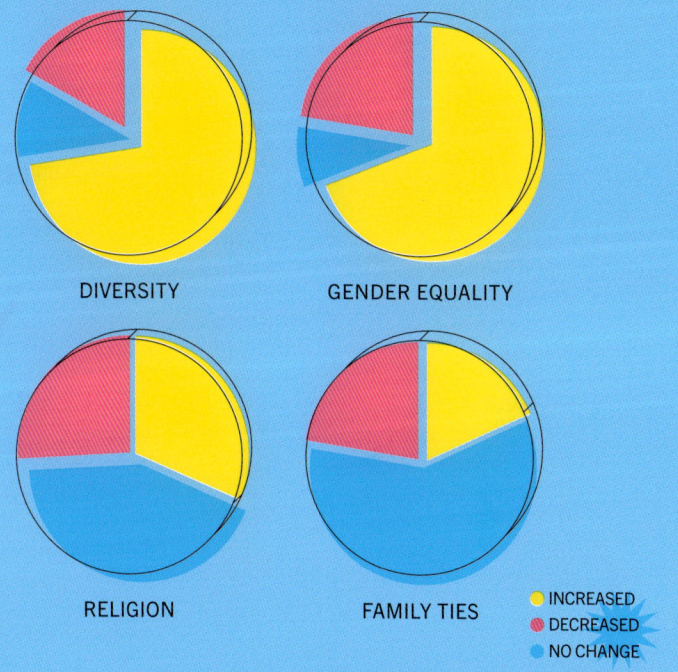

DIVERSITY

GENDER EQUALITY

RELIGION

FAMILY TIES

INCREASED
DECREASED
NO CHANGE

A 2018 Pew Research Center survey indicates that respondents in twenty-seven countries think that diversity and gender equality have increased, while connections to religion and family ties have diminished.

45

HISTORY AND GENEALOGY

Innovation is the genealogical result of many precedents coming together in a historical, material, technological, cultural, economical, and political moment.

- Brands also reflect their moment in time—they are responses to the past and present.
- A brand is a temporal meeting point.
- Since all objects and conditions are always becoming something else, brands are never fixed. They may be in the present, but that present is tumbling through time.
- An appreciation of temporality can help check one's ego and deflate the breathless bullshit of "future-proofing."
- The future is rarely what we imagined it could be. Who in the Cold War era could have imagined Mikhail Gorbachev, the last leader of the Soviet Union, appearing in a Pizza Hut commercial?
- Perhaps what that suggests is that future-proofing is either an insistence for continued momentum or resistance to change.

The first McDonald's in Moscow opened in 1990,
a year before the dissolution of the Soviet Union.

"Visual space is the space of detachment; acoustic space is tactile . . . the space of involvement." —Marshall McLuhan

- An example of such tactility can be found in auditory Autonomous Sensory Meridian Response (ASMR): a tingling sensation triggered by various stimuli.
- A person makes soft, fricative sounds into a binaural microphone: whispering, tapping, scraping, rubbing, or crumpling. The effect is maximized when listening through headphones.
- The energy of expression is important when naming a brand, but rarely addressed in any verbal guidelines document.
- One example is "Kodak," which George Eastman created because "The letter K . . . seemed a strong, incisive sort of letter." It also sounds like the click of a camera shutter.
- Whenever an orchestra or band rehearses, they focus on the attack and energy of individual notes, corresponding to the attention linguists give to phonemes. These bits of communication carry as much emotional information as the content of the text.

Autonomous sensory meridian response (ASMR) is a tingling sensation commonly triggered by specific auditory stimuli, like soft fricative sounds created by whispering, scratching, or rubbing.

47

IDENTITY

As we collectively make brand associations in our minds, brands, in return, have an equally significant role in creating us.

- Our identity is built with brands, all selected as an expression of how we see ourselves in the world.
- This identity affects how others perceive us in return. We make different assumptions about people, whether they collect manga figurines, sports memorabilia, or bongs.
- Our identity isn't a thing, but rather a collage of things.
- Given the constant flux of the market, our identity, too, is in flux.
- If all identity, both personal and brand, is made up of changing elements in a shifting universe, then authenticity is a situational agreement.
- Brands are not built. They are corralled; they are directed; they are brought into the world.

Before music streaming, a large record collection was a common method of self-expression. The collection became, in a sense, one's self-portrait.

48

INFLUENCERS ARE A RACKET

Influencers are interchangeable pieces in a race to the bottom. They are subject to constantly changing policies and terms of service of the platforms they rely on; and they are not fully vetted like celebrity endorsers.

- Media companies are developing computer-generated influencers targeted to specific demographic and regional audiences.
- These digital influencers will be twenty-two forever, free of any health issues (unless specifically programmed), and avoid controversy.
- Given the volume of influencers and the algorithmic landscape, the share of voice measured against return on investment makes influencers a questionable choice.
- They are too disconnected from a brand's authentic position to be worthwhile, unless the influencer is an authentic member of the brand's audience.
- One notable use was on the social media platform Clubhouse. The app icon changed frequently to show a user who "represents the Clubhouse community at its best" making a C shape with their hand.

This portrait of Daniel Anderson and Calista Wu, two influential users on the social media platform Clubhouse, was used in a series of app icons. In each image, the subject made the letter "C" with their hand.

49

INTIMACY

We experience non-personalized personalization every single day. It is common to receive emails that address you by name or calls that begin, "We've been trying to reach you concerning your . . . ."

- These are the result of an algorithm working within a customer relationship management platform, enhanced by research on the psychology of decision-making.
- A well-integrated system removes silos between sales, product development, and management. All groups work from the same data—whether it be operational or analytical.
- Then, ideally, product offerings become more responsive to customer behavior, messaging becomes better targeted, and waste is reduced.
- Algorithms also can add a degree of intimacy in the production or distribution process through personalization.
- But ultimately, this is not true intimacy. That comes from an investment in time and attention, which is still the domain of people.
- The goal is not to confuse real intimacy with its algorithmic simulation.

Personalized Coca-Cola
bottles with the names
Kirsty and Barry.

For a profession that claims to be concerned with forming positive connections between people, branding doesn't do itself any favors in its use of jargon. Granted, every professional group uses certain terms out of expediency or tactically. The United States Army's "MRE" is quicker to say than "Meal Ready-to-Eat."

- Branding folks are better off speaking as clearly as possible.
- Such a practice produces equally clear thinking and effective work.
- Jargon is seductive. It unites groups and helps signal competence. It also contributes to groupthink and sameness.
- "North star" is a current bit of jargon in the branding world. While evocative, consider a client having to sit through a series of presentations that all talk about finding their "north star."
- If language is a mirror of the intellect, and if the landscape of a brand is constantly fluxuating, then a rigid toolbox of jargon should be avoided.

The United States Army's "Meal Ready-to-Eat," better known as an "MRE."

51

JUNGIAN-ISH ARCHETYPES

If one constantly produces work, one develops a toolkit of strategies and resources. In brand development, one of the more persistent resources is Swiss psychiatrist Carl Gustav Jung's concept of the archetype.

- Jung believed human behavior was also informed by a collective unconscious of elements common to all human beings and laddering up into "archetypes."
- Carol S. Pearson, PhD. and Margaret Mark later proposed a set of twelve archetypes —Creator, Caregiver, Ruler, Jester, Regular Guy/Gal, Lover, Hero, Outlaw, Magician, Innocent, Explorer, Sage—working within the motivations of individuals and brands.
- This model is now quite popular. But with frequent use, it runs the danger of becoming a crutch or gimmick.
- As Mark and Pearson wrote, archetypes are "not the 'engine' of the brand . . . but [they] can be the force that accelerates the brand . . . and increases its momentum."
- Archetypes should be an inspiration and not a checklist.

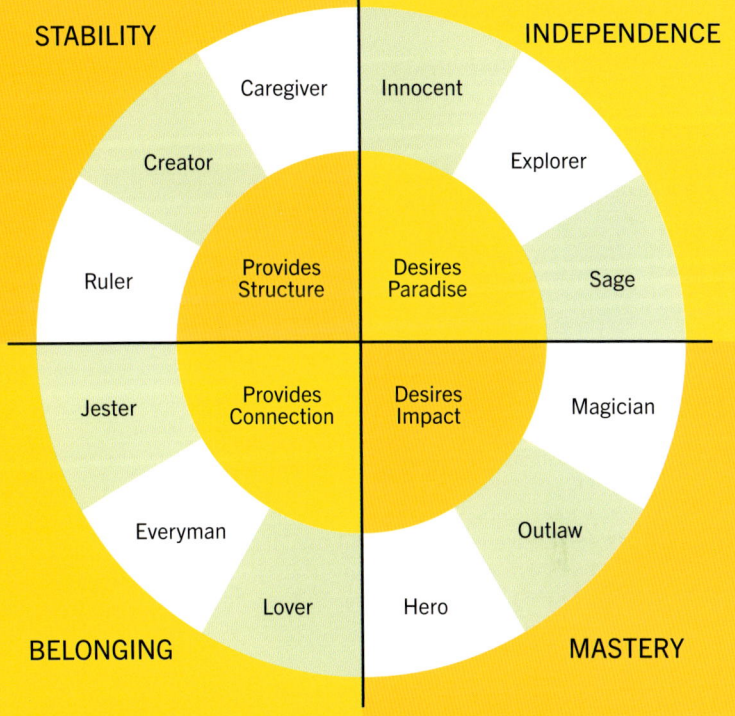

Many brand strategists use this version of Carol S. Pearson and Margaret Mark's archetype diagram.

52

KILL THE HUMAN

When presenting a brand system or advertising campaign, someone eventually asks, "Can you include a person to make it more human?"

- Besides the fallacy of asking humans, working to connect with even more humans, to make things more human, there is the commonness of such a request.
- Sadly, there are too many examples of this rationale. Wealth management campaigns show senior citizens walking along a beach in blissful retirement. Erectile medication campaigns show couples side-by-side in individual bathtubs.
- Understandably, these patterns relieve the cognitive load of continually perceiving the world. But when clichéd, they become invisible.
- One notable recent shift is the representation of people across a range of backgrounds and identities. Where it was common to see painfully obvious collections of diversity, purposeful representation seems to be receiving long-overdue consideration. This is to be celebrated.

Tropes like couples on a beach are so clichéd, they become virtually invisible.

Brands spend many hours perfecting every single aspect of packaging, regardless of how small it is. Packaging is so well-considered it inspired a whole genre of social media posts known as "unboxing."

- A theatrical first interaction/performance can act as a wonderful portal into a brand's worldview.
- It's important to remember the intended audience for these moments should be individuals.
- When it's a spectacle, like the flashy light shows on Teslas, the effect is more ego aggrandizement than personal attention.
- When an unboxing video is the point of the brand, like the L.O.L. Surprise craze of 2018–2019, the effect is cynical consumption.
- Initial interactions are opportunities to build anticipation, confirm good intentions, and strengthen brand values.
- These opportunities can go far to increase loyalty and word of mouth.

The L.O.L. Surprise doll was only meant to be unwrapped, and for that unwrapping to appear on social media. How does that benefit the consumer?

54

MAGIC AND SUPERSTITION

Looking for the perfect typeface and color is akin to believing in magic and superstition. A customer won't decide based on typographic or color details alone, or the number of values in a brand positioning.

- Desktop publishing gave designers the ability to enter text and then instantly see what it looks like in a variety of typefaces.
- A similar shift happened in color. Designers can now change colors instantly.
- With infinite variety comes the creeping anxiety of finding the perfect typeface and the perfect color palette. Designers and clients now run the danger of not being able to choose with absolute confidence, relegating them to magic and superstition.
- Data only makes things worse. Google A/B tested forty-one shades to find the perfect blue for the homepage.
- Decisions should be based on how something makes connections, rather than how it measures up to a mental ideal.

REDDIT

TWITTER

VIMEO

GOOGLE CHROME

TELEGRAM

LINKEDIN

VK

FACEBOOK

The range of blues used by eight of the social
media platforms.

55

MANAGEMENT

Developing and distributing a product or service is the collected result of more than one person's work. This merging of multiple skills and ideas requires compromise at every step.

- Even within the most collegial group, there is a need to manage and align behaviors.
- Bad brand management maintains continued vigilance over asset usage, and little else.
- While consistency is important, that is only one step toward maintaining brand coherence. The audience is intelligent enough to know that an Oreo cookie with green filling, instead of white, might be a St. Patrick's Day reference.
- Consider how Oreos might expand the brand's perception with a rainbow of filling colors.
- Meaning is not created by an unwavering constellation of brand assets. It is contextual, and it is always in dialogue with other narratives.

CHOCOLATE SANDWICH COOKIES
WITH ASSORTED CREME COLORS
NOT FOR SALE. TOTALLY FOR SHARING

Oreo cookies with differently colored fillings
developed to connect with the LGBTQ+ audience.

56

THE MASTER NARRATIVE PROBLEM

The development of consumer society needed the majority of people to agree upon matters of value, production, distribution, and control. And a good deal of that alignment was regulated through master narratives—the stories we tell ourselves, the stories we believe to be true, and the basis upon which we judge others.

- When there were fewer media outlets, the collective narrative was more coherent; aligning the audience into a mass market.
- Technological changes in communication, along with the global explosion of markets, allowed diverse voices to reach increasingly fragmented audiences.
- Public discourse(s) fractured into a multitude of historical-contextualist narratives—this added complexity to the social roles of brands.
- Earlier brands of church, school, and country built a world that, while not equitable, did much to unify humanity. Opportunities continually present themselves for us to do it again—hopefully better.

Significant historical events, like the Moon landing, can align people across political borders; as shown by these newspaper readers in Amsterdam.

57

MYSTERY IS SEXY

When business and brand strategy is formulated, logic is part of the decision-making process. And logic persists in how the brand is marketed. Saying that an alarm system equals safety is basic logic. This equals that thing.

- When an audience learns about a brand, it isn't always through a logical argument.
- The experience falls between a series of unconnected moments and is measured against a lifetime of lived experience.
- Controlling that process with a logical argument seems limiting, if not a fool's errand. You can't make someone love you through logic.
- Logical arguments close mental loops with answers and resolutions. But open loops have an element of mystery. Questions are never fully answered and the relationship goes on.
- A sense of mystery seems to be present in more successful brands. It could simply be the mystery of open questions like "Where to next?" or "Who will you become?"

Some techniques, like
the obscuring of faces,
can make an image
more interesting.

58

NAMING IS KNOWING

Knowledge through words is both possible and impossible. Names conceal and reveal at the same time.

- Naming in contemporary branding leans toward the conventional.
- Even if onomatopoeic, names need to be agreed upon. So, by default, they are conventional.
- Perhaps there's another way to think about naming a brand: write with the breath—this seems archaic, given that most writing today is done via the keyboard.
- But for the wandering lyric poets of Plato's time, as well as cultures in every corner of the world, poetry was intended to be performed in public.
- Writing with the breath adds kinetic energy—something a good namer will attend to. Poet Charles Olson said that listening to the breath "is to engage speech where it is least careless—and least logical." In other words, emotion: the domain of brand.

The name "Sonos" is relevant (reflecting the words "sound" and "sonic"), natural (the mouth becomes a resonant chamber), and when spoken, mimics the wind.

59

NOSTALGIA

Our possessions anchor us in time and place and situate us in society. As we clean out a closet or go through childhood toys, we reencounter earlier, different versions of ourselves.

- The word nostalgia is a combination of the Greek words for "homecoming" and "ache." It is usually triggered sensorially: a smell, music, an old book.
- Positive nostalgic feelings consolidate memory and make people feel connected.
- There are numerous examples of the strategic manipulation of nostalgia in advertising or product design. Vintage design motifs in Coca-Cola products, or Budweiser replacing its name with the word "America," are some of the better-known examples. All are connected with tactile objects.
- The digital order has de-objectified life and will definitely influence memory and nostalgia.
- The challenge now is how to build rich brand associations without the aid of our senses, or the effect of time on materials.

In the summer of 2016, Budweiser replaced its name on labels with the word "America." The remainder of the text used phrases from the Pledge of Allegiance and lyrics from "The Star Spangled Banner" and "America the Beautiful."

The chemicals that allow printed material to appear on a bright white surface in vivid colors are all pollutants. Their presence, while invisible to the user, remains in the environment.

- A focus on the first impression, the sale, the packaging has had an equally harmful effect for over a century.
- This effect extends into pretty much everything beyond printed ephemera.
- Sustainability is an increasing concern for producers and consumers alike. Phrases like "cradle to cradle" describe a mindset where garbage becomes a resource in a production chain. But a chain that still begins with a natural resource.
- Who says that the purpose of branding is only to get people to buy shit they don't need?
- If branding can unify people, what if it also extolled the virtues of producing, consuming, and having enough?
- The continuity of life on earth is probably the most urgent brand today.

Products purchased online may magically appear at the door, but their production and delivery have environmental effects.

61

OBSERVATION

Strategists analyze consumer or market behavior across two broad categories: quantitative or qualitative.

- Quantitative, or "quant," examines data pulled from a large sample size. The questions asked tend to be highly structured and specific because the goal is to collect numerical data, which is then subject to statistical analysis.
- Qualitative surveys place researchers directly into the area of study. They investigate individual motivations with open-ended questions (never a "yes" or "no") and the ability to ask follow-up questions specific to the respondent.
- It's easy to think of quant and qual as binaries at extreme points along a scale. One is numbers, while the other is narrative.
- But the two types of data are both incomplete descriptions of an object.
- Consumer insights are not just about the consumer at a moment in time. They are about both the consumer and the business acting within a larger ecosystem.

Can liminal states, like distraction, fit into the analysis of market or customer behaviors?

62

ONE _____ FALLACY

Over time, it's natural for an organization's structure to become complex and fragmented. Brands can either undergo a brand architecture project—a complicated assessment, reorganization, and repositioning that might take more than a year and may alienate internal stakeholders—or they can announce an initiative with the name "One (name of the company)."

- The One _____ direction rarely results in effective change. There is no well-defined call to action, ideal state, or unifying theme. Just saying that an organization is One _____ doesn't make it so.
- The one effective result of a One _____ initiative is pointing out an organization that should consider taking a closer look at their brand.
- To anyone with a degree of experience in branding, One _____ is most likely a temporary fix. Because strong, effective associations are rarely made by edict.

Top: Logo designed by Milton Glaser for a 1977 campaign to promote tourism in New York State.

Bottom: 2023 version of the 1977 campaign, created for the Partnership for New York City.

63

OUT OF HOME, BUT IN THE MIND

As traditional magazine readership and broadcast viewership declined and technological innovations upended basically everything, the advertising industry has been forced to change in every way.

- The line between brand and advertising has become blurred.
- One advertising sector in that space is out-of-home (OOH): billboards, posters, bus stops, spots found within public transit, actual storefronts, and an amorphous category known as either alternative or guerilla.
- Things become interesting when a brand's normal behavior becomes an ad for itself. For example: Tesla's Light Show illuminates all the lights on the car and can open the trunk and windows, all choreographed to music on the sound system.
- Tesla does not do traditional advertising. Seeing their showrooms is all the marketing required. And there is a halo effect from company chairman Elon Musk's other activities in SpaceX, solar energy, battery development, and social media.

Tesla superchargers act as OOH advertisements for the vehicles.

64

PARODY IS A SIGN OF SUCCESS

A November 2013 commercial for Volvo trucks featured action star Jean-Claude Van Damme. In it, Van Damme performs one of his trademark splits, suspended between two Volvo trucks. It was an audacious spot—and a perfect target for parody.

- Soon after, animation firm Delov Digital's holiday greeting showed fellow action star Chuck Norris doing a split between two flying airplanes, with several men balanced on his head in the shape of a Christmas tree.
- Such references are known as earned media.
- It used to be the exclusive domain of publicity and news reports, but in the digital realm, earned media now includes Yelp reviews, TikTok reels, and any other appearance in social media.

Jean-Claude Van Damme performing one of his trademark splits during a 2017 press conference in Munich, Germany.

65

PARTY PEOPLE

The image of a salesman going door-to-door is archetypal and the subject of countless jokes and cartoons. But over time, social mores, algorithms, and COVID-19 have transformed the profession to the point where it exists more in a business-to-business (B2B) context than a direct-to-consumer one.

- Instead of armies of door-to-door salesmen, we now have experiential marketing. It could be as viral as an "influencer" ordering a new liquor at a bar, then speaking to the people next to them about the product. Or it could be a temporary pop-up shop or a hospitality tent at a larger event.
- Regardless of the scale, such experiential marketing really only meets the "awareness" stage of the customer journey.
- If anything, people will more likely remember the party and not the brand.

An early example of experiential marketing is the Wienermobile, used to promote and advertise Oscar Mayer products in the United States. The first vehicle was created by Oscar Mayer's nephew, Carl G. Mayer, in 1936.

Each brand, like each person, has a distinctive personality. But rather than immediately diving into specificities and differences, sometimes it helps to step back and think in a wider manner. A good approach is to look for the more open-ended aspects of the brand by asking what it allows.

- There seems to be longevity in permission. Permission maintains open territory for future growth, where regulations and restrictions do not. Permission makes room for what otherwise would be considered off brand.
- For example, Kraft Mac & Cheese has offered brand extensions into Mac & Cheese–flavored gummy candy, ice cream, and candy.
- Permission allows one to say, "Yes." Obviously, we don't say "yes" to everything, but keeping an open mind to opportunities for a brand to flourish is certainly a growth mindset.
- Such a mindset is less about consumption and more about the gift of possibilities.

Clockwise from top left: Kraft Mac & Cheese main product packaging, collaboration with Van Leeuwen ice cream, and Kraft Mac & Cheese prepared with a candy flavor packet to turn the mac & cheese pink and add hints of sweet candy flavor.

If one wanted to distill branding into a single word, that word would be "framing." The more distinctive the framing, the more effective the brand. Positioning a brand benefits from "lateral thinking." Such thinking avoids classic A+B=C logic in favor of intuition, humor, and play.

- Lateral thinking disrupts routine approaches and allows for a wider variety of inputs and associations.
- In corporate structures, unintegrated play resists being accounted into billable hours, thus framing it as unprofessional behavior. What client would pay for "playtime?"
- Instead, teams attempt to manage the chaos of unintegrated thinking into a regulated game known as brainstorming.
- Brainstorming is the opposite of play. Participants moderate their contributions based upon their perception of agency and power. The word itself—"ideation"—carries the expectation of a tangible product at the other end of the process.

Brainstorming is the opposite of play. There is a political order to the process, which reinforces routine approaches and results.

All human activity lives amongst a variety of other activities. Each reflects a political reality.

- Regardless of their intention, brands express a political position.
- Today, that position has never been more transparent or documented—this condition is full of both peril and opportunity.
- The risk is in aligning with a figure or cause which can backfire.
- There are "comfort food" positions as well: aligning with a cause that doesn't require too much thinking, or cause controversy. These actions may satisfy the board's desire to take a stand without really taking a stand, but they have little longevity. It's a quick hit of satisfaction but doesn't do much to gather people into the brand's "tribe."
- Aligning an audience into a political sphere can resonate longer than many touchpoints. For example, the Pepsi Generation continues to exist. We may not know what it means, but we know how it makes us feel.

Z Y X W V U T S R Q P O N M L K J I H G F E D C B A

It's time to look at things differently.
Again.

Starbucks advertisement
originally developed in
2002 by Thomas Prowell.
The tribute runs annually
with slight revisions to
the text. This version says
"It's time to look at things
differently. Again."

PROFESSIONALISM SECOND

Professionalism is responsible for the improvement of all methods and processes and the very thing hindering that progress. Because it is a standard against which compensation and reward is evaluated; we need to be wary of its pitfalls.

- Professional domain expertise frequently leads to "siloization."
- The value of one's work is tracked through notoriety, profit, and attention, which all contribute to a sense of professionalism. This external feedback is easier to measure and appreciate, but it can limit as well.
- Brands unite many domains: history, economics, politics, culture, and language. They are interdisciplinary, and their development should be as well.
- If someone outside your domain makes a suggestion or asks an "uninformed" question, try not to see it as an attack but rather as a gift. It is an opportunity to clarify, reach outside your silo, and make that connection.

"Siloization" prevents true collaboration and reinforces the norms within each professional domain.

Designed objects are the mediators of human relationships. We sit in (designed) chairs, around (designed) tables, over (designed) meals, and engage with others.

- Branded objects and, at a larger scale, brands themselves mediate human interaction.
- Keeping this in mind opens an opportunity for brands and branding professionals to view their audience as more than a means to an end (aka, a source for profits and returns).
- Then why is our system of production so geared toward the bottom line? Short-term returns come at the expense of long-term relationships, which is counter to the relationship-building ethos of branding.

French architect Jean Nouvel's intention for the Louvre Museum in Abu Dhabi was to create "a welcoming world serenely combining light and shadow, reflection and calm." It also "emphasizes a fascination with unusual discoveries" of Middle Eastern and European aesthetics.

71

RENDER UNTO CAESAR

We are so used to seeing advertising in public that it exists in an almost liminal state: not quite conscious nor unconscious.

- There are times when advertising—New York's Times Square or Shibuya Crossing—creates a certain aesthetic thrill. Such locations establish who we are as a community and create a collective manner of expression.
- And there are situations when such a cacophony becomes an eyesore, provoking governmental regulation.
- The need to legislate advertising and signage stems from landscapes ruined by rapacious consumerism.
- But advertising, signage, and logos are part of our collective heritage.
- A question in the Bible asks if one should pay taxes to Caesar. The response—give to Caesar what is Caesar's, give to God what is God's—is a both/and situation. Balancing the needs of the brand with the needs of the public can solidify bonds between the brand's audience and the community.

Current state of the Queens Place Mall, in Elmhurst, Queens, New York City. Designed in 1965 by Skidmore, Owings & Merrill, one of the most significant architectural firms in the world, it now has an unfortunate collection of disproportioned logos on the façade.

72

REPAIR AND AGE

Because they are associated with marketing, brands are also tied to the idea of the new and improved. The dopamine hit at purchase or upon first use is limited to the beginning of one's relationship with a brand. Getting new things just feels good.

- As products become more complex, producers argue that their coding and development now fall under intellectual property law. So, if a car needs repair, the owner is required to bring it to a dealer.
- There is growing social and legislative pressure for the consumer's right to repair.
- The production and distribution of reparable products or products that improve with age (leather goods being a great example) can have a beneficial effect for a brand. It reduces supply chain pressure, is sustainable, and suggests the company isn't trying to squeeze every bit of profit from the consumer.

Blue jeans communicate externally to other people, as well as back to the wearer. And that message is colored by the wear and tear of continual use.

73

REPETITION AND SYNCOPATION

We wear clothing every day, but we don't feel it because its familiarity to our skin doesn't demand our attention. But if it's ill-fitting, itchy, wet, or on fire we notice.

- Familiarity can work for a brand. Disney parks disguise nonthematic structural elements like ductwork, fencing, and towers with two proprietary colors: Go Away Green and Blending Blue. Both are close enough to the colors of the landscape and sky to go unnoticed.
- The challenge is to deliver a familiar brand experience in a way that allows each customer to feel seen as an individual. This could be through a variety of interactions, sequences, or styles.
- The musical term for this is syncopation: a displacement of a regular beat creating a sense of anticipation or forward movement. Robotically delivering the same experience becomes dull quite quickly. Even consistent brands like Coca-Cola change their packaging occasionally.

Disney's proprietary colors disguise nonthematic structural elements.

Top: Go Away Green on the structure's roof.

Bottom: Blending Blue on the retaining wall.

74

RETINAL / NON-RETINAL

Artist Marcel Duchamp defined "non-retinal" art while speaking about Andy Warhol: "If you take a Campbell's soup can and repeat it fifty times, you are not interested in the retinal image. What interests you is the concept that wants to put fifty Campbell soup cans on a canvas."

- Duchamp's non-retinal concept offers a lesson for visual designers. If one looks at design trends at any point in time, the similarity between pieces and brands is remarkable.
- This is because the majority of designers relegate themselves to the retinal. They serve the eye, which in turn satisfies the ego.
- Their innovations are celebrated in industry awards, which build studio reputations, and ultimately attract clients.
- But every trend eventually goes out of style.
- Instead of chasing new trends, why not pursue non-retinal branding systems? The results will definitely be surprising and may create even deeper brand associations.

In 1915 Marcel Duchamp selected a snow shovel as a readymade, titling it "In Advance of the Broken Arm." This, on the other hand, is a snow shovel, photographed with retinal intent.

Photo: Myers Creative Imaging.

161

75

RITUALS AND ROUTINE

It's not uncommon for brands to be associated with some sort of a ritual. As the objects in our lives situate us in time and culture, the rituals that we engage in make time livable. Ritual is not about production or consumption. It is about being fully present and fully in the moment.

- Supreme sneaker drops and Harry Potter midnight book releases are about consumption, which is tied to a production and marketing schedule. They are more routine instead of ritual.
- Routine may give structure to time—like a morning Starbucks— but it does not symbolically connect individuals and community. This is not to say that brands are automatically exempt from meaningful rituals. For example, since 1924, Macy's has hosted the Thanksgiving Day Parade in New York City.
- Distinctions between ritual and routine are worth keeping in mind when proposing brand behaviors.

Traditions like
the regalia of the
Household Troops and
the Changing of the
Guard ceremony at
Buckingham Palace
contribute to the brand
known as Great Britain.

A scope is an enhanced estimate defining every step of the branding process. While every project is different, it is helpful to have a few generalized strategies.

- Avoid just designing a logo. Anything less reinforces misperceptions about branding.
- In long-term partnerships, consider proposing a basic time-and-materials approach.
- Break the scope into discrete phases to establish benchmarks and billing phases.
- Any research done before winning the project falls outside the scope.
- The open secret in branding is even the biggest firms deploy small teams on their largest global clients. If you are a smaller agency, consider using this fact to your advantage.
- Charging a percentage of the total fee (6 to 8 percent) for basic expenses and local travel is worth asking for. Nobody likes receipts.
- A client may think a too-round number wasn't properly calculated. Learn from retail: $14.99 is better than $15.00.

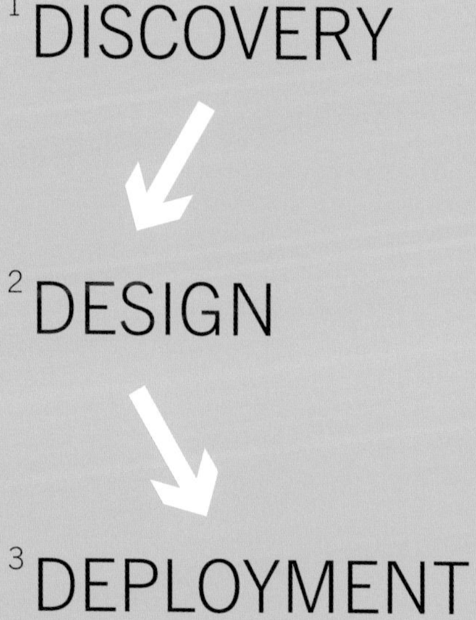

¹ DISCOVERY

² DESIGN

³ DEPLOYMENT

Writing a scope of work with three basic phases of discovery, development, and deployment establishes evaluation benchmarks and billing thresholds.

The absorption of trademarked names into common vocabulary is basic human behavior, and the struggle of intellectual property lawyers. Parker Brothers may have trademarked "Ping-Pong," but the word defines any back-and-forth exchange.

- The term for this is "semantic infiltration."
- This is not limited to language. The effects of products extend to our behavior, future products, and so on.
- When Sony introduced the Walkman portable cassette player, people's relationship to music and technology changed almost immediately. The Walkman allowed users to select exactly what they listened to and create playlists for specific activities. One could have specific music for workouts, commuting, or shopping. And one could communicate via mixtape.
- By giving us control over our audio environment—to the point where people no longer pay the sort of attention to music that they used to—the Walkman changed the way we perceive our world.

The first Sony Walkman, the TPS-L2, was released in 1979 and forever changed the way we perceive our world.

The establishment of brand associations in the mind is done through a process, known in semiotics, as a sign.

- Philosopher Charles Sanders Peirce saw a sign as a three-step process. It begins with the object (Peirce's naming convention), which is anything thinkable. The object is represented in a manner—a word, image, gesture, etc.—that can be interpreted. Finally, that representation is decoded, or interpreted.
- If the interpretation aligns with the object, that is a closed semiosis. But if it does not align, then that can become a second representation, which sets up a new interpretation: ad infinitum. This is known as an open semiosis.
- Why does this matter to branding? Simply put, a sign (or brand) does not exist unless it is acknowledged as a sign (or brand).
- This realization shifts the branding process from monologue to dialogue.

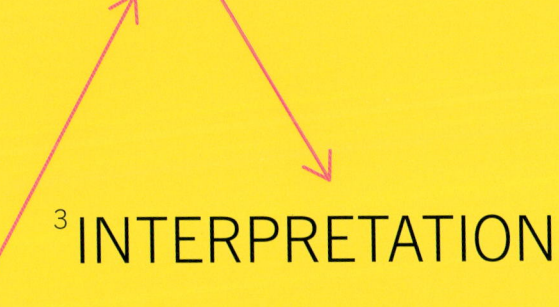

²REPRESENTATION

³INTERPRETATION

¹OBJECT

Charles Sanders Peirce's model of a sign as a
three-step process, also known as a "semiosis."

Currently, branding has a branding problem. It is frequently seen as a profit-driven practice that motivates people to adapt inauthentic ideas, pursue false aspirations, and consume more. But human activity is concerned with more than buying and selling—and so should branding.

- So why do branding firms defer so easily to client whims?
- The average tenure of a marketing executive is only a few years. Constant churn rewards highly-visible rebrands over brand integrity. A new chief marketing officer joins a company, and subsequently begins a new initiative, ending in a new logo, a new name, and a new positioning.
- Compounding this are profit requirements incentivizing agencies to create that new logo, name, and positioning.
- Branding firms insist that a brand is more stable than a campaign, but their willingness to take on these projects suggests that they don't believe what they preach.

 1970–1986

1986–October 4, 2010

October 4–11, 2010

October 11, 2010–January 2016

January 2016–present

Evolution of the Gap logo. The 2010 iteration was
so widely criticized, the company reverted to the
previous version after a week.

SOCIAL RESPONSIBILITY

Because of their role in culture, brands are caught in the middle of social conflict. Social fracturing, compounded by the immediacy of social media, means that a brand can no longer hide.

- After his protest of racial inequality, no NFL team would sign American football player Colin Kaepernick.
- The following year, Kaepernick appeared in a Nike ad with the text, "Believe in something. Even if it means sacrificing everything."
- When Nike celebrated American independence with an American flag motif, Kaepernick publicly pointed out the country's history with slavery. Nike quickly pulled the product, prompting criticism from conservative political voices.
- There is no easy approach to how a brand addresses social responsibility. A positively received move one day can lead to a long-term decline later on. The one certainty is that brands need to look beyond just financial return and think deeply about their role in society.

An electronic billboard for Nike products featuring Colin Kaepernick, the American football player who knelt during the national anthem as a protest of police brutality and racial inequality.

In the 1970s, a generation of German musicians developed a music style known as Krautrock. A notable component was the 4/4 "motorik" drumbeat. The motorik beat expressed a technological future full of possibility, and a cosmopolitan sensibility.

- If a logo and visual identity system can signal the feeling of a brand, then so can a drumbeat.
- Current sonic branding is generally harmonic or melodic: Brian Eno's 1995 startup tone for Microsoft Windows or Chase Bank ATM feedback cues.
- Mercedes-Benz vehicles are engineered to make a reassuring, solid "thud" when the door closes. While not music, the thud is still composed.
- The possibilities for sonic cues are endless—succeeding or failing, depending on context.
- Snapple Iced Tea bottles make a distinctive pop when opened, suggesting freshness. The pop lost its context when Snapple switched from glass bottles to plastic. Now the product doesn't quite taste the same.

Klaus Dinger from the band Neu! on drums, 1970.
Superimposed: the basic Motorik beat.
Photo: Wolfgang v. Groote.

STANDARDS

Corporate identity is the standardization of a company's visual assets into a unified look and feel.

- The output of graphic design studios in the mid-twentieth century is considered the golden age of corporate identity. The standards manuals produced during that time gave specific instructions on constructing a company's visual identity to the smallest detail.
- With the advent of branding, the territory for standards manuals is expanding beyond the visual, and even beyond tone of voice and writing standards. It is not uncommon for a financial institution's credit card design standards to address the strategies behind those cards. Environmental design standards—even though every space is different—will define materials and approaches, down to the choice of decorative plants. And customer interaction may not be specifically definable, but there can be a company-wide approach.
- Today's brand standards need to move beyond strict rules into empowering appropriate decisions.

In 2014, Standards Manual published a reissue of the 1970 *New York City Transit Authority Graphics Standards Manual*, originally designed by Massimo Vignelli and Bob Noorda of Unimark International.

Few can confidently define strategy and its role. The leading definition comes from the American economist Michael Porter, who wrote: "... strategy is about being different ... deliberately choosing a different set of activities to deliver a unique mix of value."

- But how does one go about being different? Perhaps we need a better definition.
- Strategy is a two-pronged activity: one analyzes an existing context, and then proposes a new context intended to meet goals.
- There are four degrees of strategy:
  - Management consultants who develop overall operational strategies.
  - Next are the "upfront" strategists who create a moment of punctuated equilibrium where perception changes.
  - Sometimes a strategist helps sell creative work.
  - At the most detailed level is "donkey work." This is where reams of material is compiled and processed for the previous three levels. It may not be the most glamorous, but it is vital.

The American economist and professor, Michael Porter.

A logo is a mnemonic device that triggers a brand association. Verbally, a tagline has a similar function. For lack of a better term, a tagline is a verbal logo.

- A tagline, or strapline, is a short phrase capturing the essence of a brand's character.
- A slogan is a summarizing phrase in a marketing campaign.
- A slogan can become a tagline, and a tagline can be used as an advertising slogan.
- One of the most-admired taglines, Nike's "Just do it," began as an advertising slogan.
- The phrase applies to both internal and external audiences and aligns with the company's mission.
- "Just do it" then informs the criteria when designing product packaging (easy to open), websites (quick to load), or products (does not constrict movement).
- Goldman Sachs' entry into consumer banking used the line "you can money." There is no stated promise of capabilities, access, or results, just attitude.

Nike's "Just do it," began as an advertising slogan and eventually became a call for everyone, regardless of ability, to be physically active.

85

TAKE ME HOME

A brand's intimate relationship to its customers must remain under continual adjustment. Computer technology distills large amounts of data into sharp insights, which are acted upon by algorithms, bots, and customer relationship management software (CRM).

- Every interaction has become an opportunity for a sale. The message is "buy me."
- The default of "buy me" puts branding in a cynical light.
- Once one purchases a new bed, how necessary are follow-up emails promoting a new bed, which is the exact same bed?
- On the other hand, what if messaging moved from the transactional to the propositional? Instead of "buy me," wouldn't it be better to say "take me home." It's difficult to think of a more intimate sentence.

Russ Meyer 🇺🇸 🏳️‍🌈 🌻 🇺🇦
@russhmeyer

· · ·

CRM is why I'm getting birthday greetings from companies I haven't
frequented in years.
Thanks??

6:42 PM • Jan 29, 2022

This tweet by American brand strategist Russ Meyer
captures the false sense of intimacy generated by
customer relationship management software.

86

TALK TO THE GATEKEEPERS

A pop-up shop, or a temporary retail venue, can be an ideal way to test out or introduce new products, a brand extension, or a co-branded partnership. Its ephemerality creates a bit of drama, and, if done well, there can be a halo effect as well.

- Previously, pop-ups were best opened where influential news and publishing channels were headquartered: urban centers like New York City, Los Angeles, or London. Having a concentrated audience of editors, writers, and producers maximized the effect.
- With print and broadcast's demise, and the rise of the digital realm, locations with more specific demo- and psychographic profiles came to the forefront.
- This was Brooklyn, Shoreditch, or Oberkampf: hip neighborhoods teeming with influencers.
- Social media influence is hard to predict, and any alignment with a cool neighborhood can quickly be seen as inauthentic—a menu selection rather than a genuine alignment.

The cult beauty brand Summer Fridays teamed with Upside Pizza in New York's SoHo for a pop-up, featuring food and limited-edition apparel in March 2023.

When one thinks of Tiffany & Co., the robin's-egg blue of the packaging comes to mind. One doesn't even have to see the logo to think "Tiffany."

- Tiffany Blue only means Tiffany because of its consistent usage within context. Seeing an egg that color would make most people think "robin," not "Tiffany."
- When presenting color palettes, why do people justify their choices by ascribing psychological or symbolic attributes? These attributes are rooted only by cultural association and have no inherent meaning.
- Black may be the color of death in the West, but in Asia death is white.
- To insist on one-to-one correlations between colors and meaning isn't considering historical or cultural antecedents.
- Christian Louboutin shoes trace back to Louis XIV, who ruled only those in royal favor could have red heels on their shoes. The specific meaning may have changed, but the use is similar.

Red soles on a pair of Christian Louboutin shoes.

Since branding is such a varied process, it seems appropriate to address how disciplines interact and identify a useful approach in managing diversity.

- The geodesic dome serves as an ideal model.
- The structural principle keeping the dome up is known as tensile integrity.
- Nothing is twisted or torqued. Once everything is in place, the mutual and distributed pressure upon all elements strengthens the overall structure.
- Mutual pressure and tension define the ideal relationship between strategy and design. It is best if everyone is detached from their ego and focused toward the benefit of the project. In this environment, "I think blue is too close to our competition's color palette," is better than "I don't like blue."
- All comments and suggestions have to be qualifiable.
- Disagreements can be gifts. Objections show that an idea is being considered. And being asked to explain oneself strengthens the idea.

The mutual and distributed pressure upon all
elements of a geodesic dome strengthens the
overall structure, which can then efficiently cover
wide areas without the need for columns.

"Word art" is inspirational and motivational language writ large on a wall, on a mass-produced pillow, or in your Instagram feed.

- WeWork locations had "Love what you do" on walls and staff T-shirts. Starbucks locations feature a neon sculpture that reads "Coffee = togetherness." And there are numerous iterations of "Live, laugh, love" available in every big-box houseware stores.
- It might seem logical for brands to consider displaying their taglines, values, or mottos in an equally elevated manner.
- Philosopher Slavoj Žižek points out that such text is "wisdom instead of proper thinking." It may sound deep but is more like intellectual comfort food.
- These platitudes and bromides are bits of nonthinking. Thinking is open-ended, allowing for varieties of expression, multiple methods, and diverging conclusions. Word art shuts down thinking.
- Besides the intellectual suppression, word-art wisdom is becoming another item on the brand-building checklist.

Platitudes writ large, like this neon sign that reads "Make it Happen," are moments of nonthinking.

The structure of a recipe is simple: a list of ingredients and a step-by-step process. But upon reflection, time is more than just a procedural step; it is truly a transformative ingredient. One adds it in the correct proportions, like flour, salt, or anything else.

- After a 1986 demonstration at a proposed McDonald's location in Rome, the Slow Food movement was founded. Their manifesto claimed "under the sign of Industrialization . . . Speed became our shackles . . . 'the fast life' . . . fractures our customs and assails us even in our own homes. . . ."
- Currently, the Slow Design movement advocates for the deceleration of resource consumption and production.
- Both groups see society's focus on productivity as contributing to environmental and cultural decline.
- Therefore, slow creativity—let's call it Slow Branding—might help shift the development and distribution of brands toward the mutual health and success of producer, audience, and environment.

The Slow Food Condotta Valle Ossola agricultural education project near Domodossola, Italy.

TOUCHPOINTS

English-speaking branding professionals describe every opportunity for a brand to enter someone's consciousness with the word "touchpoint."

- Touchpoints are more than the moments of purchasing, delivering, and opening. They also comprise liminal moments of awareness: hearing about it in passing, or seeing a logo out of the corner of your eye.
- Watching a friend open an app on a smartphone is a touchpoint. Seeing a roadside sign for a restaurant or arranging to meet someone in front of a shop are also touchpoints.
- Brand touchpoints can have a crucial role in the valuation of a company.
- Even if one applies a small amount of value to every liminal, casual perceptive moment of any trace of a brand's presence, one quickly sees the cumulative value of brand touchpoints—and the effect of brand on a company's overall value.

Even a brief reflection
of a T-Mobile logo
glimpsed in the window
of a Reebok store
counts as a touchpoint.

If the price someone is willing to pay is driven by an abstraction like value, then a brand's impact on a company's value seems logical.

- Brand value is impossible to measure objectively.
- One simple method is to assign a modest, singular value appearance of a logo on all touchpoints. For example, if done for an international bank, that would include logos on all signage, webpages, credit cards (bank issued and co-branded), statements, advertisements, promotional materials, tote bags, ATM receipts, and so on.
- If one values each appearance modestly—say, 50 cents to a dollar—the total would be in the millions, if not billions, of dollars.
- Global consumer brands that sell merchandise would have an even higher valuation. Imagine the cumulative perceptual effect of all T-shirts sporting Mickey Mouse, across all possible contexts.
- That, in itself, has significant financial impact on a brand's value.

Actor Wilmer
Valderrama in a Mickey
Mouse T-shirt at the
The Dukes of Hazzard
premiere, in Grauman's
Chinese Theatre,
Los Angeles, CA, on
July 28, 2005.

197

VALUES

In describing a hammer, one can list its shape, size, weight, and the materials of its manufacture, as well as where a hammer is commonly found.

- These qualities are incomplete unless we know what the hammer is used for—in this case, striking another object so the hand is not harmed.
- A standard procedure in brand development is establishing a support system of values for which the brand stands. These are (or should be) an expression of the brand's purpose and can be projected into any length of time.
- For example, the dating app Hinge's stated goal is to be deleted. If they are successful, users won't need the app anymore.
- Consider defining brand values simply, with an end goal (or purpose) and a support system of values designed to clear the space needed in order to reach that end.

The values and goals of a hammer's potential use determine its final form.

If a brand is attentive, its presence in popular culture may present opportunities to expand into new territories and markets.

- In hip-hop culture, luxury brands signified rebellion and transcendence. But brands like Gucci didn't produce the sizes, silhouettes, or styling that the audience wanted, nor were they easily accessible.
- Couturier Daniel Day, aka Dapper Dan, printed patterns of appropriated logos, sometimes mixing different ones on the same garment. And as his clientele's fame grew, he drew the attention of trademark lawyers. After years of raids and lawsuits, Day closed shop in 1992.
- At a 2017 Gucci fashion show, Alessandro Michele presented a jacket resembling a 1989 Dapper Dan model. After accusations of cultural appropriation, Gucci declared it an "homage." Several months later Day opened a studio for custom clients with the raw materials supplied ("powered") by Gucci.
- The copier was now the copied—and an equal partner.

A U.K. Gucci advertisement featuring Daniel Day, known as Dapper Dan.

WAR LANGUAGE

Two traditions give us the modern branding professional: the atelier, originating in the workshops of artisans; and the office, which evolved in governments and trading companies. Their influence echoes in the language of branding.

- The atelier sharpened the eye, refined individual touch, and developed one's taste. Its apprenticeship system established a baseline upon which subsequent generations could innovate.
- The office tradition was built around the mind; seeing the world as a collection of reserves and resources. The goals were acquisition, growth, and profit.
- The origins of the office lead to a militaristic tone pervasive in modern branding. The goal is to win accounts and acquire territories.
  - "How did the presentation go?"
  - "We killed it."
- But the language of the atelier, the studio, speaks of relationships, alignment, centering, and proportion.
- Ways of speaking can help set an empathic approach to one's audience. Because words are the first expression of thoughts.

Top: The atelier, where traditions, materials, and processes are united.

Bottom: The office, which sees the world as a collection of reserves and resources.

In 2017, a United flight departing from Chicago was fully booked. To make room for company staff, travel vouchers were offered to anyone willing to vacate their seats. None of the paying passengers accepted.

- Passengers were informed that four of them would be displaced.
- Three agreed to leave. The fourth, Dr. David Dao Duy Anh, politely refused to deplane. Security officers were called to remove him, knocking him unconscious in the process. They then dragged him out past passengers, some who were recording.
- Once footage hit social media, there was wide public outroar. United's stock prices fell and preference polls indicated flyers would be willing to spend more not to fly United.
- In one event, five decades of United Airlines' "Fly the Friendly Skies" brand campaign was rendered worthless.
- Until we reward compensation with metrics other than efficiency and profitability, that mindset will remain every brand's weakest link.

When brand benchmarks focus on profit and not people, the results can resemble this 2021 protest during the UN Climate Change Conference in Glasgow, Scotland.

In the book *In Praise of Good Bookstores*, Jeff Deutsch writes, "The good bookstore sells books, but its primary product, if you will, is the browsing experience."

- The bookstore encourages repeat visits and lingering. When the customer's sensibilities align with the environment, a sense of community is present.
- This extends to lifestyle brands like Ralph Lauren. Whether through distressed jeans, velvet suits, house paint, or sportswear, the brand grounds its customers within a vague historical lineage, which then burnishes how they see themselves.
- This is why bookstores, and now Ralph Lauren shops, have cafés.
- In effect, these brands are selling a way to use time itself.
- This is a fascinating extension of branding: the manner in how one spends time is a brand.

The Ralph Lauren flagship store in New York's Upper East Side now has a café; where customers can spend time in a Ralph Lauren manner.

When a product, or collection of products, represents a group mindset so efficiently, it becomes a lifestyle brand.

- Martha Stewart is a classic example. There is a Martha Stewart way to bake a cake, to mix a cocktail, to decorate a home, to dress . . . and a Martha Stewart way to enjoy that cake and cocktail, in that home, while wearing those clothes.
- There are no limits to what can be absorbed into a brand, no disciplinary boundaries.
- So, if there are no limits to what comprises a brand, then something so insignificant as a hashtag can be a brand.
- #blacklivesmatter groups are like-minded people under a shared vision of the world they would like to live in. It is world-building, just like any other lifestyle brand.
- And it efficiently describes an individual with as much precision as Martha Stewart or any other lifestyle brand.

The Black Lives Matter brand grew beyond its American origins into a global phenomenon, as shown in this June 2020 image from a demonstration in London.

99

YOU ARE NOT A BRAND

Let us distinguish between "brand" and "personality."

- We all have a friend who sticks out somehow: always running late, loves manga, or wears all black. And when speaking about their behavior, we might say they were either "on brand" or "off brand."
- And some of us might know a person claiming to be "working on my brand," when in reality they are going to school, making TikToks, or updating their resumé.
- These two examples show how the word "brand" has detached from its marketing origins and is now floating freely in everyday usage.
- Like individuals, brands have personalities. And those personalities help distinguish the associations held in people's minds.
- Individuals become brands when their associations involve more than a handful of people.
- Barack Obama connects with a progressive social agenda. And when he speaks, we're moved to action because of our emotions, not by his argument or personality.

Barack Obama's association with cultural and political groupings evoked different brand-level responses.

Top: An Obama rally held the day before the 2012 election in Madison, Wisconsin.

Bottom: An anti-G20 protest on November 15, 2014, in Brisbane, Australia.

100

ZANY, CUTE, AND INFORMATIVE

Since brands are "consumed," some attention should be paid to the aesthetics of their consumption.

- Theorist Sianne Ngai proposed that the categories reflecting today's society are the zany, cute, and informative. They correspond with how we produce, consume, and choose.
- The zany resonates with the precariousness of modern work. As any Amazon employee can attest, the modern workplace demands more productivity with fewer resources.
- The cute describes the power relationship between consumer and consumed. From Hello Kitty to E.T. and, counterintuitively, to Freddy Krueger, rendering something as cute is how we empower ourselves when facing the world.
- The informative isn't fully comprehensive, but just informative enough to allow us to maintain existing patterns. We prefer to appear informed, but end up making emotional decisions.
- Public discourse limits our aesthetic engagement with the marketplace. Since aesthetics trigger emotions, this explains the limited palette of our expressive spectrum.

Two examples that conform to Sianne Ngai's description of empowerment through "cute."

Left: A sexy *Nightmare on Elm Street* Halloween costume.

Right: Hello Kitty band-aids.

ABOUT THE AUTHOR

Mark Kingsley is a creative director and strategist with a wide range of experience and recognition. As Executive Strategy Director at Collins, he developed the new global positioning for Ogilvy and helped Equinox enter the luxury hotel business. At Landor, Mark was the global creative lead on the Citi account—overseeing design, intranet development, workshops, and global brand audits. Additionally he was part of Ogilvy's Brand Innovation Group (BIG), created Hewlett-Packard advertising for Publicis & Hal Riney, and designed fragrance packaging at Cosmair.

For over 17 years, his studio Greenberg Kingsley specialized in music and arts, creating years of branding and advertising for Central Park SummerStage; products for the Guggenheim Museum store; and music packaging for Blue Note Records, John Coltrane, Pat Metheny, Quincy Jones, Ginger Baker, Jewel, and Yes. His work received a Grammy nomination, and was selected for AIGA 50 Books/50 Covers.

He previously held the endowed Melbert B. Cary Professorship in Graphic Arts at the Rochester Institute of Technology. His approach to brand strategy fuels the work of his current studio, Malcontent (malcontent.com), working with global brand agencies, feature film directors, and fashion startups.

In 2016 he was profiled in *Print* magazine as one of "56 Inspiring Designers Shaping Our World Today." And he was a subject of professor Alice Twemlow's PhD thesis, published in 2017 by MIT Press as *Sifting the Trash: A History of Design Criticism*.

ACKNOWLEDGMENTS

A thinking life begins with influential teachers. Mine include Robert C. Morgan, R. Roger Remington, Ajay Singh Chaudhary, and Mihai Nadin.

An experienced life requires colleagues and clients. My global network at Landor, friends in various agencies and studios, and my art world/music industry clients opened many doors, opportunities, and perspectives.

Ideas need a place to live. My eternal gratitude to Debbie Millman for building the Masters in Branding program at the School of Visual Arts in New York City, and for clearing a space for me to grow. My fellow faculty and students graced me with inspiration, encouragement, opposing ideas, and suggestions worth pursuing.

Writers need readers. Thank you to Dr. Tom Guarriello, Dr. Brad Davidson, Melinda Welch, Kristin James, Kelsy Postlethwait, Michael Shirey, Mikel Rouse, and Jane Brown for their feedback and encouragement. And my deepest thanks to this book's de facto dramaturge, Lisa Sheridan, who read everything, workshopped half-baked ideas, and helped bang everything into a proper shape.

Books need publishers. Thank you to my editor Jonathan Simcosky for his eternal patience and encouragement, and thank you to the staff at Quarto/Rockport for their additional patience and energy.

I have been blessed with caring and supportive family members and friends—some long passed, some recent additions. This book is a testament to your love.

ALSO AVAILABLE:

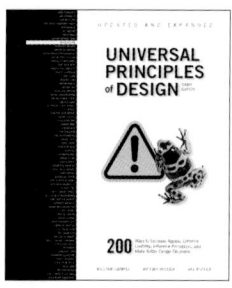

Universal
Principles of Design
(9780760375167)

Universal Principles
of UX
(9780760378045)

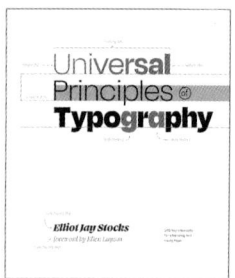

Universal Principles
of Typography
(9780760383384)

Universal Principles
of Architecture
(9780760380611)